Dan Burley's
Jive

Dan Burley's Jive

Edited by Thomas Aiello

NORTHERN

ILLINOIS

UNIVERSITY

PRESS

DeKalb

Dan Burley's Original Handbook of Harlem Jive
Originally self-published, 1944,
by Dan Burley
New York, NY

Diggeth Thou?
Originally self-published, 1959,
by Dan Burley
Burley, Cross, & Co.
Chicago, IL

Library of Congress Cataloging-in-Publication Data
Burley, Dan, 1907–1962.
[Dan Burley's original handbook of Harlem jive]
Dan Burley's jive / edited by Thomas Aiello.
    p.   cm.
The book combines into one easily accessible volume two works:
Dan Burley's Original Handbook of Harlem Jive and Diggeth Thou?
Includes bibliographical references.
ISBN 978-0-87580-623-5 (pbk.: alk. paper)
1. African Americans—Languages. 2. English language—Slang.
3. African Americans—Commumnication. 4. Black English.
5. Americanisms. I. Aiello, Thomas, 1977– II. Burley, Dan, 1907–1962.
Diggeth thou? III. Title. IV. Title: Jive.
PE3727.N4B87 2009
427'.97308996073—dc22

for Madison

CONTENTS

INTRODUCTION

Thomas Aiello

"Jive," wrote Dan Burley in 1944, "is language in motion." His *Dan Burley's Original Handbook of Harlem Jive* didn't create jive slang, but throughout the 1940s it fostered it, popularized it, broadened its use beyond the cloister of the jazz community. It acted as an invisible conduit of the new urban linguistics to the "square" world.

Of course, even the most dogged of linguists inevitably reach a threshold on the known origins of various idioms, American or otherwise. No one, for instance, could ever pin down just who first sat in the pleasant company of friends and deadpanned, "Okay, so a guy walks into a bar . . ." They could discover its first use in copyrighted print, but for phrases and idioms based on the spoken word—be they jive talk or parlor jokes—written precedent is only tangentially beneficial.[1] Burley, for his part, placed the original American use of jive in the early 1920s. It was "a distortion of that staid, old, respectable English word 'jibe.' . . . In the sense in which it came into use among Negroes in Chicago about the year 1921, it meant to taunt, to scoff, to sneer—an expression of sarcastic comment." His is an authoritative voice, and his account seems plausible. But his conclusions are based on experience, not research. Written precedent remains ineluctably elusive.[2]

Still, linguists have had much to tell us since Burley's original publication. In 1976, Eric Townley argued that the continued and various uses of the word *jive* between 1935 and 1945 gave it so many different meanings that the word itself was "almost meaningless unless within the context of a sentence." Like Burley, Townley guessed that the word's origins came from the English *jibe*. He counted it as defining subjects as various as music, dancing, marijuana, slang, or sex. Townley, too, located the genesis of much of this speech in 1920s

Chicago, the jazz nightlife, poverty, and segregation creating an atmosphere whereby such language could be "absorbed."[3]

Scholars originally assumed that the development of African American slang came as a result of faltering attempts by slaves to learn the language without proper instruction. But scholars working in the later twentieth century have discovered many African origins for such words. David Dalby has noted that the African Wolof word *jev* means "to verbally disparage" someone. In the Cameroon language Efik-Ejagham, the word *jiwe* means "monkey," and is often used as a representation of trickery. Debra DeSalvo argues that jive was an original form of coded communication used by African slaves. With African tongues banned by masters (and, in many cases, colonial governments), jive was a modified form of English that allowed slaves to stay within linguistic rules while still maintaining the ability to carry on clandestine conversations.[4]

This theorizing on the African origins of *jive* is telling. The whole of the lexicon that Burley would have placed under the larger cope of jive language has been the subject of extensive linguistic study over the second half of the twentieth century and into the twenty-first. Take, for example, the word *cool*. The calm, confident, soulful person that is—in Burley's America or ours—"cool," is in West African Yoruba culture *itutu*, which designates a person's "ability to connect with one's inner divinity." This concept, too, like the various permutations of *jive*, came to the American colonies on African slave ships. The Wolof word *hipi* signals someone's awareness and vision. The suffix *-kat* designates a person. The combination, a "hipi-kat," is a person who understands the goings on around him/her—a "hepcat," in Burley's linguistic paradigm.[5]

The Wolof, from western Senegal, became victims of the seventeenth-century religious tumult fed by attempted Christianization of the African continent from the west and Muslim influence from the east. After an attack by an Islamic sect, the

Wolof first fell victim to slave traders in the 1670s and would continue coming to the colonies until the mid-eighteenth century. Their constant contact with English speakers for such a sustained amount of time necessarily gave them a heady influence on the language. Now-common English words like *banana, bug,* and *yam* came from the Wolof. The group's word for singer, *katt,* is said to have influenced the jive term *cat* to describe an accomplished, hip musician.[6]

Still others have argued that the transfer of specific words and phrases is less important in understanding the full force of African cultural transfer than are syntax, grammatical structure, and "communication style." It is, they argue, the form of African American speech that demonstrates a connection to Africa, rather than any specific word. Emphasis on simple vocabulary, in this formulation, causes the researcher to miss the forest for the trees.[7]

Far more beneficial than written precedent, however—to both the historian and the linguist—are the most influential, popular, or revelatory uses of a new idiom or language group. Dan Burley's *Handbook,* published in 1944, and *Diggeth Thou?* published in 1959, were all three. Burley's influence on American speech is undeniable. As Earl Conrad notes in his foreword to the original edition of Burley's *Handbook,* "He who interprets Dan Burley could prophesy the language, the thinking and the people of some future America that I know is on the way. I know it is on the way because Dan is a symptom of it." The profusion of hip-hop culture and slam poetry in the early twenty-first century, along with the general celebration of all things urban, belies a vast array of dependencies on the "cats" and "chippies" of the 1940s and '50s. Dan Burley was the "gasser of jive spiel" among them, and his work played an integral role in the creation of the modern language.

Geneva Smitherman has noted that every language reformulation by African Americans (or, for that matter, by any dispossessed group) is fundamentally more than the linguistic cubbyhole "slang" describes. The term *slang* signals a temporary lack of concern. But the manipulation of words—for the original African arrivals, for Burley and his peers, and for the hip hop generation of the late twentieth and early twenty-first centuries—carried with it a broader frustration and social critique that was not intended to be temporary. The semantic critique of hip hop, then, owes a number of debts to the language of Burley's day. First, many of the words themselves have survived. Burley's jive wasn't temporary slang. It was a bedrock shift in the language of the dispossessed. Second, hip hop's dependence on African culture and contemporary music as the two dominant wellsprings of new linguistic creation mirror the actions of Burley and his counterparts. It is a borrowing of both language and method.[8]

H. Samy Alim has similarly located the language of modern hip hop in a combined "creolization" and sociopolitical critique. Alim finds in "Hip Hop Nation Language" the same core elements employed by Burley, such as the use of the call and response. Both hip hop language and jive also manipulate the traditional definitions of words to claim them for a minority community (and, as a consequence, to demonstrate the power of such linguistic malleability). Both hip hop and jive demonstrate a narrative sequence rooted in the long tradition of black storytelling. Both emphasize the power of rhyming and "multi-textual collage-style composition." Both co-opt traditional white forms (for Burley it was Keats, Shakespeare, "The Night Before Christmas," etc.).[9] In all of these efforts, linguistic innovators attempt to cordon off a unique language to combine the common elements of a certain portion of society. At the same time, a core constituent of that language is its ability to change and be changed. Malleability, then, becomes the seedbed of black speech, and "Hip Hop Nation Language" becomes the necessary evolutionary outgrowth of jive.[10]

Of course, any account of Burley's influence on language would be incomplete without an account of his own influences. Much of this verbiage can be seen in the poetry of the Harlem Renaissance. "The life of the Negro people is not simple," wrote Richard Wright in 1937. "The presentation of their lives should be simple, yes; but all the complexity, the strangeness, the magic wonder of life that plays like a bright sheen over the most sordid existence, should be there. To borrow a phrase from the Russians, it should have a *complex simplicity*."[11] Perhaps no one embodied that complex simplicity more than Langston Hughes, particularly in his early, mid-1920s poetry.

> Droning a drowsy syncopated tune,
> Rocking back and forth to a mellow croon,
> I heard a Negro play.
> Down on Lenox Avenue the other night
> By the pale dull pallor of an old gas light
> He did a lazy sway . . .
> He did a lazy sway. . .[12]

In the title poem of his 1926 *The Weary Blues,* Hughes not only emphasized the musicality of urban speech (and, in particular, black speech), but he did so in the language of jive.[13] Of course, the poet was less concerned with cramming his work with as many representations as possible of the new hip vernacular. But the new hip vernacular was there, nonetheless. Like Burley, he sought to represent a real, uncensored Harlem life. Unlike Burley's, Hughes's vernacular led early to critical hand-wringing. Twenty years before the publication of the *Original Handbook of Harlem Jive,* the gatekeepers of black literature were unprepared for Hughes's use of jazz language and his depiction of the jazz nightlife. As Richard K. Barksdale has noted, Hughes and his fellow poets of the Harlem Renaissance embodied the influences of jazz, blues, and indigenous

African primitive culture, often to critical frowns. But poetry and music, according to Hughes, were both for and of the "low-down folks."[14] And in the culture wars of urban black America in the 1920s, Hughes would win.

There would be similar imagery in the poetry of Claude McKay—

> I hear the halting footsteps of a lass
>   In Negro Harlem when the night lets fall
> Its veil. I see the shapes of girls who pass
>   To bend and barter at desire's call.[15]

And in the songs of Bessie Smith—

> I ain't high yeller, I'm a deep killa brown
> I ain't gonna marry, ain't gonna settle down
> I'm gonna drink good moonshine and run these browns down.[16]

The literary significance of presenting the perceived heart of urban culture with the language that permeated the streets became paramount to authors of the Harlem Renaissance. "We younger Negro artists who create now intend to express our individual dark-skinned selves without fear or shame," wrote Hughes in 1926. "If white people are pleased we are glad. If they are not, it doesn't matter. We know we are beautiful. And ugly too."[17] In the coming decades, Dan Burley would epitomize this new emphasis on the unvarnished expression of African American life and speech.

Daniel Gardner Burley was born in Lexington, Kentucky, on November 7, 1907. His father was a former slave and Baptist minister, his mother an educator who served under Booker T. Washington at the Tuskegee Institute. He moved to Chicago as an adolescent, and there he cultivated a talent for writing and jazz piano.[18] Burley began writing for the *Chicago Defender* between 1925 and 1928, while he was still attending high school according to some accounts. After leaving the weekly newspaper, he traveled the country, making his living through odd jobs and piano playing before returning to write for the *Chicago Bee* in 1932. He acted as sport and theater editor and columnist for the *Bee*, while simultaneously working as a correspondent for the Associated Negro Press, but a contractual dispute in 1937 convinced him to move to New York. At the *New York Amsterdam News*, Burley edited the city, sports, and theater pages. His "Back Door Stuff," a social gossip column, often featured jive writing, developing a style imitative of the inner-city speech Burley heard in Chicago and Harlem.

In 1944, he published *Dan Burley's Original Handbook of Harlem Jive*, a dual representation and linguistic analysis of that speech, including short stories, poems, and translations of classical and Shakespearean literature into jive. He located its origins in early 1920s Chicago and used the created language to emphasize the social and economic plight of those in the inner city. The *Handbook's* combination of cultural critique and language manipulation drew the admiration of a wide range of readers, from Nation of Islam leader Elijah Muhammad to journalistic curmudgeon and linguist H. L. Mencken to Langston Hughes himself.

Though it was unique in the field, however, the *Handbook* did owe much to a series of precursors that also attempted to compile the language emanating from the nation's jazz clubs and inner cities. "[The Negro's] very words are action words," wrote Zora Neale Hurston in 1934. "His interpretation of the English language is in terms of pictures . . . One act described in terms of another. Hence, the rich metaphor and simile." In her "Characteristics of Negro Expression," Hurston provided an early academic examination of black speech. The emphasis of Negro syntax on action and the creation of verbal pictures led to its insistence on the power of metaphor. Black speakers' distinct impact on broader American grammar came first from its use of "double descriptive" phrases like "chop-axe" or "more better," she noted, and second from their creation of verbs from common nouns ("funeralize," for example, or, "She features somebody I know"). It was a speech based on baroque embellishment and action, always action. Unlike later linguists, Hurston didn't find the roots of this expression in African linguistics. Instead, she saw it as a reformulation of inherited white speech, a sort of crib of the language that fed back into the mainstream after its unique modification. The intricacy of her analysis spread to the formulation of "Negro dialect," noting the black tendency to drawl the personal pronoun "I," and the selective drawl of repeated words. "This is particularly true of the pronouns. A pronoun as a subject is likely to be clearly enunciated, but slurred as an object."[19]

Hurstson's work was not a catalog. It was an evaluation. But it gave way in the following years to a series of compilations that sought a more objective listing of the new urban vocabulary. Carl Cons's 1935 "The Slanguage of Swing: Terms the 'Cats' Use" began the systematic program of collecting and defining jazz slang terms. Linguists Russel B. Nye and H. Brook Webb came up with similar lists for a 1937 edition of the journal *American Speech*. Finally, in 1938, scat musician Cab Calloway published *Cab Calloway's Hepster's Dictionary*.[20]

Less systematic projects began even earlier. In 1926, Carl Van Vechten published *Nigger Heaven*, a novel about a romance between an elevator operator (and aspiring writer) and a librarian. More broadly, the novel was about life in Harlem and the racism that acted as its overarching circumference. Van Vechten's portrait was intended to be an accurate portrayal of Harlem. To that end, along with the virtuous protagonists, beset by the trials of a world they couldn't change, the novel also included a number of less virtuous characters—prostitutes, racketeers, bootleggers. The language, too, was meant to be as representative as possible. "Oh, gaze on dat wobble, man!" "If you've never been vamped by a brown skin . . . Too skinny! Ain' she loose! Jelly-roll lak mine!" At the end of the novel, Van Vechten includes a brief glossary to explain some of the more exotic terms. "Happy dust" was cocaine. "Dogs" were "feet. Not to be confused with hot-dogs, frankfurters inserted with mustard between two halves of a roll."[21]

Two years later, Rudolph Fisher published *The Walls of Jericho,* his first of what would be many novels. Fisher was a doctor by trade, an educated man who wrote in his debut about the trials faced by black professionals living at the intersection of the white and black worlds. A black lawyer buys a house in a white Manhattan neighborhood adjacent to Harlem and finds in the imaginary lines that divide the two areas a "wall of Jericho." Fisher's account, like Van Vechten's, was a realistic portrayal of Harlem life and speech, and, to that end, Fisher also included "An Introduction to Contemporary Harlemese, Expurgated and Abridged."[22]

It is these accounts, far more those of Hurston, Cons, or Nye and Webb, that provide a direct legacy for the work of Dan Burley. Like *Nigger Heaven* and *The Walls of Jericho,* Burley's project veers from such cataloging efforts in its attempt to use that collected language in creative fiction and poetry. That said, however, both the *Original Handbook of Harlem Jive* and *Diggeth Thou?* are unique in their trajectory and purpose. The seeming inscrutability of the language itself is the Wall of Jericho Burley seeks to destroy. Whereas the novels seek a cursory explanation of certain words to enhance the story preceding them, Burley's work is designed to enhance the language itself. Jive is the cause, not the consequence, of the stories contained within. It is intended to entertain as much as it is intended to edify.

Throughout his career, however, Burley was known predominantly as a sportswriter. His sportswriting was often more intense and direct than was his experimentation with jive. The man of jive metaphor found the state of sport itself to be a metaphor for the Jim Crow status quo. And so he became an activist through his columns. His accounts often lauded athletes that impressed him but turned critical at perceived injustices. Burley argued vehemently for baseball's integration throughout the early 1940s and used sports as an example of the need for desegregation in all facets of American life. During the war, he criticized boxer Joe Louis for fighting in a racist navy and railed against the 1942 detention of Joe DiMaggio's Italian immigrant father. After baseball integrated in 1947, he vigorously denounced the racist epithets hurled at Jackie Robinson, Larry Doby, and others. Burley's sportswriting led him to become the first African American member of the New York Boxing Writers Association.[23]

In 1951, Burley returned to Chicago to serve as associate editor of the Johnson Publishing Company's *Jet* and *Ebony* magazines. *Jet* was an understood "spinoff" from *Ebony* that appeared the same year Burley arrived in Chicago, and he is sometimes credited with the idea for the popular periodical. He stayed at the Johnson publications until 1957, then briefly acted as managing editor for the new black weekly, *Chicago Crusader*. Burley's financial situation, however, became more and more tenuous as the 1950s wore on. He never again earned the salary he received in New York. In the last years of his life, he again worked for the *Defender* and created his own weekly paper, *The Owl*, along with freelancing for a variety of white mainstream publications. Declining salaries and a growing family prompted him in 1959 to write a sequel to his *Handbook, Diggeth Thou?*[24]

He self-published the book and even sold the manuscript on the streets of Chicago. The text of *Diggeth Thou?* demonstrates that though the circulation did not match that of the *Handbook,* Burley was still able to enunciate the jive language that made his name. Fewer were listening, but the message remained strong and competent. Unlike his earlier work, *Dig-geth Thou?* did not bother with semantic analysis of the jive phenomenon. Instead, it offered poetry, prose, and parodies presented in Burley's signature jive style. He notes in the preface his struggles in producing a second book, and the volume's soliloquies on poverty and drug abuse clearly indicate the author's struggles to succeed in the urban world his writing celebrated.[25]

The toll of editing and writing—and the toll of creeping poverty and possible drug abuse—had given Burley a heart attack in the late 1950s, and doctors and friends encouraged him to lighten his workload. He ignored the advice, and on October 29, 1962, he died of a second heart attack.[26]

Clarence Major argues in his introduction to *Juba to Jive: A Dictionary of African-American Slang* that "black" speech is not categorically correlative to "street" speech. He would not deny, however, that modern African American slang, be it "street" or otherwise, is functionally dependent on rural/slave language, jazz/bebop language, and all other variants that came before it. Major also describes the information culture (and its attendant inclusiveness) that has eliminated many of the linguistic and racial barriers of the past. In 1967, Stewart Berg Flexner described the development of slang as a rejection of mainstream culture, a culture that users of slang were excluded from, anyway. It was, in effect, a defense mechanism. The early twentieth-century linguist James Hart credited popular music with acting as a conduit for jive slang into the broader culture.[27]

Certainly, Hart and every examiner of the period has pointed to jazz as the source of much of the "jive talk" present in Burley's work. Carl Cons described a variety of different word categories under the broader heading of "jazz language": specific musical terms, derisive words describing classical musicians, words for good and bad jazz fans, and a significant number of drug references.[28] Burley's jive incorporates many of these terms but ventures far afield of jazz terminology. He wasn't enunciating a vernacular of jazz culture. He was enunciating a vernacular for Flexner's dispossessed—for Hughes's and Hurston's dispossessed—the rejects from mainstream "white" culture, replete as it was with economic imperialism and Jim Crow hypocrisy.

African American slang is now part of American language, and thus its growth is integral to the growth of the entire semantic system. Interestingly, Burley's introduction to the *Handbook* credits the formation of jive to the intermingling of the races. "Although jive originated among Negroes, it has no color line. In fact, jive has broken down quite a few barriers of race itself." The "hepcats" and young adults began viewing themselves within categories such as "jazz" or "social outcast," and thus began using speech that cordoned them off from the well-off "square" world. Earl Conrad notes in his forward to the original edition of Burley's *Handbook* that "anyone who could interpret Dan could establish the magic link between the Negro and the white worlds; he could show us how and why one world influences the other, why the two are constantly merging in myriad ways." This was the age of the Beat Generation, who incorporated jazz slang into their speech and writing and helped define the literature of the age. Lawrence Lipton suggested that the beats used the vernacular as a rite of passage, a form of initiation into an exclusive club. Being "hip," and thus knowing all of the intricate speech patterns and rules of those similarly hip, was a passcode into that cloistered cool world. The same seems to be true for Burley's jive.[29]

But Burley's work dealt specifically with an urban African American version of the broader "jazz slang." And his experimentation with jive was neither silent nor inarticulate on the question of race and civil rights. The insistence of its message is equivalent to the one he presents in his sportswriting. "Diggeth Thou? (Mose on the Lam from Egypt, Alabam)" may be one of the most potent essays on the state of race relations in the 1950s South ever produced. In the late chapters of the *Handbook* and throughout *Diggeth Thou?* Burley veers away from his original formulation of jive and emphasizes the blackness of the vernacular. His frustration with the progress of African American civil rights and the crushing poverty of inner-city New York and Chicago is clearly evident.

"Like in the wheel within a wheel," writes Burley in the title work of his second compendium, "this is the deal that went down in the little old town of Egypt Alabam where Mose hit a grand slam by taking the Israelites on the lam." The piece is a forceful retelling of the biblical exodus story, placing the "Israelites" in the heart of racist Alabama. Like much of his work, Burley's depiction has important antecedents emanating from the pages of the Harlem Renaissance. Zora Neale Hurston's *Moses, Man of the Mountain* tells the same story. Though her novel doesn't use American place-names like "Alabam," it does signify its civil rights significance through the use of African American dialect. Both begin with the troubled situation of Moses's birth and carry the story through slave freedom. Of course, Burley's tale is less than 2,500 words and is attempting a linguistic feat with which Hurston is largely unconcerned. Hurston, then, is able to spend an introductory chapter emphasizing the persistence of the exodus story in African and Asian cultures. She is able to develop fuller characters. (Moses, for example, finally comes to the realization at the end of Hurston's novel that "no man may make another free. Freedom was something internal." Freedom for Burley's Moses is always an external, active event.)[30] Still, the two stories are doing the same work, and the immediacy of Burley's short account compensates for its lack of narrative depth.

"Diggeth Thou? (Mose on the Lam from Egypt, Alabam)"
also owes a debt to Langston Hughes's "Christ in Alabama."

> Most holy bastard
> Of the bleeding mouth,
> Nigger Christ
> On the cross
> Of the South.

Hughes portrays the Alabama slave as the product of the
dominating power of white masters and the matriarchal legacy
of black mothers. "Christ is a nigger," he writes, "Beaten and
black." He turns the southern black population into the sac-
rificial lamb that could redeem the white South, thus leading
to a different sort of exodus. The imagery in Hughes is clearly
from the New Testament, but the core elements of righteous
indignation, white suffering, and black tribulation combine
with biblical imagery to denounce the apartheid system in
twentieth-century Alabama.[31]

And so the *Handbook,* and *Diggeth Thou?* in particular, were
works of civil rights advocacy, but other elements of the work
require warning for those accustomed to politically correct
speech. The *Handbook* and *Diggeth Thou?* are not as potentially
abrasive to mainstream readers as, say, Iceberg Slim's 1969
Pimp: The Story of My Life, but the two works remain similar
in other ways. Both are exposés of the black urban situation,
and both can be seen as important civil rights documents.
But both deal openly with drug abuse, and both are rampant
with sexism. In the *Handbook* and *Diggeth Thou?* "chickens"
and "hens" and "chippies" are valued for their age (the closer
to sixteen, the better) and their shading (the closer to white,
the better). In *Diggeth Thou?* one piece argues that spousal
violence is often necessary and beneficial. African Americans are "spades," Latin Americans are "spics," and Asian

Americans are "squints." Homosexuality is derided and marijuana use is advocated (and, in a later *Diggeth Thou?* tale, cocaine enters the plot). It must be remembered, however, that Burley's words (as did Slim's) reflect both the speech and the mind-set of the Harlem and Chicago of his day. It is their accuracy that should make the largest impression, not their "uncensored mode."[32]

This emphasis on drug culture is telling. Burley's work, like much of the best writing of the same era, was intended to be *experienced*. This introduction, then, will leave further semantic analysis, discussion of syncopation and rhythm in the urban vernacular, or the jazz musicality of jive linguists to other works.[33] The author offers his own analysis of the history, technique, and meaning of jive in the *Handbook*, and his opinion is the one of principal importance to this volume.

The illustrations, too, are important. Melvin Tapley illustrated *Dan Burley's Original Handbook of Harlem Jive*, and Frank Lee illustrated *Diggeth Thou?* In 1944, when the *Handbook* first appeared, Tapley had been working for the *New York Amsterdam News* for two years, where he trained under Bill Chase. He would stay until his retirement in 1998. His comic strips included *The Brown Family, Jim Steel, Spoofin', Dos & Don'ts,* and *Breezy*. Lee was born Eugene Rivers in Spartanburg, South Carolina, in 1926. Five years after illustrating *Diggeth Thou?* Lee changed his name again, becoming Eugene Majied. A devoted member of the Nation of Islam, Majied would never use the pseudonym Lee again. He became a cartoonist for the group's newspaper, *Muhammad Speaks*, and served in that capacity through the rest of the century.[34]

Finally, an editorial note is in order. The "Jiver's Bible," which originally appeared at the close of the *Handbook*, now appears at the close of the entire volume. Explanatory and editorial notes appear where necessary. While some commas, capitalizations, and quotation marks have been added for clarity, and typos have been removed, the text largely retains its original form.

Clarence Major argues that slang, unjustly, "has never had a consistently good reputation," but that it is "intrinsic ... to the quest of human culture to express and renew itself."[35] Whether Dan Burley was the creator of jive, or simply one of its most influential proponents, his contribution to modern American language proved pivotal to Major's understanding of cultural renewal. Language moves like trains through a city, getting to every end only with the aid of stops along the way that are integral to both the trains' motion and people's ability to harness that motion for their own purposes. Burley's work—in the *Handbook, Diggeth Thou?* and his "Back Door Stuff" column in the *New York Amsterdam News*—served as one of those central points of access. And though the debt remains largely unacknowledged, vast communities of Americans still arrive in the public sphere on trains emanating from Burley's stop.

NOTES

1. That said, there is, in fact, written precedent. The *Oxford English Dictionary* notes Louis Armstrong's 1928 recording "Don't Jive Me" as one of the first documented cases of *jive*'s verbal usage. It also appeared that year as a noun in Rudolph Fisher's *Walls of Jericho,* the first of his novels and a defining work of the Harlem Renaissance. *Oxford English Dictionary*, 2nd ed., vol. 8, *Interval—Looie* (Oxford: Clarendon Press, 1989), 245. See also Louis Armstrong and His Hot Five, *Don't Jive Me,* audio recording, Columbia 36376, 1928; and Rudolph Fisher, *Walls of Fisher* (Ann Arbor: University of Michigan Press, 1994).

2. Linguist Robert S. Gold has expressed a similar frustration at the inability of researchers to find first sources. He noted that this vernacular was even more difficult to pin down than most other colloquial jargon because of its roots in jazz and jazz culture—"groups in our society least likely to record their acts and thoughts in writing." Robert S. Gold, "The Vernacular of the Jazz World," *American Speech* 32 (December 1957): 275.

Introduction

3. Townley cites Mezz Mezzrow's *Really the Blues* as a telling account of the interracial 1920s Chicago jazz nightlife, including its close association with racketeering and more criminal elements of Chicago culture. See Mezz Mezzrow, *Really the Blues* (New York: Citadel Press, 1990; originally published 1946); and Eric Townley, *Tell Your Story: A Dictionary of Jazz and Blues Recordings, 1917–1950*, x, 178–79.

4. Debra DeSalvo, *The Language of the Blues from Alcorub to Zuzu* (New York: Billboard Books, 2006), xiii, 95; David Dalby, "The African Element in Black English," in *Rappin' and Stylin' Out: Communication in Urban Black America*, ed. Thomas Kochman (Urbana: University of Illinois Press, 1972), 171; and Joseph E. Holloway and Winifred K. Vass, *The African Heritage of American English* (Bloomington: Indiana University Press, 1993), 143.

5. DeSalvo, *The Language of the Blues from Alcorub to Zuzu*, 45–46, 81; and Holloway and Vass, *The African Heritage of American English*, 139.

6. Music transfer from Africa to the New World was just as influential—perhaps more so—than linguistic transfer. DeSalvo and others have discussed the role of the African "griot" and his relationship to the community. For a sustained study of African musicality and its relationship to the blues and other American musics, see Alan Lomax, *The Land Where the Blues Began* (New York: New Press, 1993); and Paul Oliver, *Savannah Syncopators: African Retentions in the Blues* (New York: Stein and Day, 1970). For more specifically on the role of the "griot" in African culture, and the surrogate musicians in the United States, see Oliver, pages 43–52. DeSalvo, *The Language of the Blues*, xiv, 34; Samuel Charters, *The Roots of the Blues: An African Search* (New York: Da Capo, 1991), 59; and Holloway and Vass, *The African Heritage of American English*, 137–83.

7. Molefi Kete Asante, "African Elements in African-American English," in *Africanisms in American Culture*, ed. Joseph E. Holloway (Bloomington: Indiana University Press, 1990), 19–33.

8. Geneva Smitherman, *Black Talk: Words and Phrases from the Hood to the Amen Corner* (Boston: Houghton Mifflin, 2000), 3, 22–25.

9. H. Samy Alim, *Roc the Mic Right: The Language of Hip Hop Culture* (New York: Routledge, 2006), 10; and Imani Perry, *Prophets of the Hood: Politics and Poetics in Hip Hop* (Durham: Duke University Press, 2004), 8, 58–101.

10. Alim, *Roc the Mic Right*, 69–108. See also, Tricia Rose, *Black Noise: Rap Music and Black Culture in Contemporary America* (Hanover, NH: Wesleyan University Press, 1994).

11. Wright's statement, ironically definitive of Depression era black writing, was actually part of his turn away from the movement generally known as the Harlem Renaissance, as he sought a far more politically engaged black authorial project. His "Blueprint for Negro Writing," from which the above quote comes, was originally published in *New Challenge* 2 (March 1937): 53–65. It has been reprinted ad infinitum. This quote comes from *The Harlem Renaissance: A Brief History with Documents*, ed. Jeffrey B. Ferguson (Boston: Bedford/St. Martin's, 2008), 172–77.

12. Langston Hughes, "The Weary Blues," originally published 1926. Reprinted in *The Langston Hughes Reader* (New York: George Braziller, 1958), 87.

13. Though we see this emphasis most readily in Hughes's early work, it also existed later in his career. In *Montage of a Dream Deferred* (published in 1951, at the height of Burley's success), Hughes sounds much like the hipsters populating the juke joints of Harlem and Chicago.

> Good morning daddy!
> Ain't you heard
> The boogie-woogie rumble
> Of a dream deferred?

Langston Hughes, "Dream Boogie," in *Montage of a Dream Deferred*, originally published 1951. Reprinted in *The Langston Hughes Reader* (New York: George Braziller, 1958), 89.

14. Richard K. Barksdale, *Langston Hughes: The Poet and His Critics* (Chicago: American Library Association, 1977), 16–17, 20, 24–25. See also Steven C. Tracy, *Langston Hughes and the Blues* (Urbana: University of Illinois Press, 1988).

15. Claude McKay, "Harlem Shadows," *Pearsons Magazine* 34 (September 1918): 276.

16. Bessie Smith, "Young Woman's Blues," originally published in 1926, republished in *The Harlem Renaissance: A Brief History with Documents*, ed. Jeffrey B. Ferguson (Boston: Bedford/St. Martin's, 2008), 123.

17. Langston Hughes, "The Negro Artist and the Racial Mountain," *Nation,* 23 June 1926, 692–94.

18. That love for piano led to a later jazz recording career, where he cultivated a sound he referred to as "skiffle." After recording with Lionel Hampton in 1946, Dan's Circle Session produced an album featuring songs such as "South Side Shake" and "Lake Front Blues." A later session for Arkay Records produced "Chicken Shack Shuffle" and "Skiffle Blues." See Dan Burley, *South Side Shake, 1945–1951,* CD, Vienna: Wolf Records, 1991, WJB-CD-008. Burley also performed with Dizzy Gillespie on the latter's 1947 feature *Jivin' in Be-Bop.* Burley teamed up with Johnny Taylor to perform "Hubba-Hubba Blues" and "Boogie in C," numbers interspersed between performances by Dizzy Gillespie and His Orchestra. See Dizzy Gillespie, *Jivin' in Be-Bop,* originally published 1947, DVD, New Orleans: Storyville Records, 2008, B00114XTFC.

19. Zora Neale Hurston, "Characteristics of Negro Expression," in *African American Literary Theory: A Reader,* ed. Winston Napier (New York: New York University Press, 2000), 31–34, 43–44.

20. Of course, such attempts are ongoing. See DeSalvo, *The Language of the Blues;* and Townley, *Tell Your Story.* Carl Cons, "The Slanguage of Swing: Terms the 'Cats' Use," *Down Beat* 2 (November 1935): 1; Russel B. Nye, "Musician's Word List," *American Speech* 12 (February 1937): 45–48; H. Brook Webb, "The Slang of Jazz," *American Speech* 12 (February 1937): 179–84; Cab Calloway, *Cab Calloway's Hepsters Dictionary* (New York: self-published, 1938); and Rick McRae, "'What Is Hip?' and Other Inquiries in Jazz Slang Lexicography," *Notes* 57 (March 2001): 574–84.

21. Carl Van Vechten, *Nigger Heaven* (New York: Alfred A. Knopf, 1926), 249, 282, 285.

22. Rudolph Fisher, *The Walls of Jericho* (Ann Arbor: University of Michigan Press, 1994; originally published New York: Alfred A. Knopf, 1928), 295–307.

23. For a compilation of selections from Burley's sportswriting, see Jim Reisler, *Black Writers/Black Baseball: An Anthology of Articles from Black Sportswriters Who Covered the Negro Leagues* (Jefferson, NC: McFarland, 1994), 127–44.

24. Burley's first wife, Gustava McCurdy, was a concert singer and the first black woman to sing the "Star Spangled Banner" in Madison Square Garden. After her death and Burley's return to Chicago,

he married his second wife, Gladys, the manager of a Chicago school bus company. Gladys brought to the new family two children from a previous marriage, Sharon and Peter. In 1952, Dan Burley's only child, D'Anne, was born.

25. There are drug references throughout the *Handbook,* as well, but they are limited to marijuana and do not depict dependency. *Diggeth Thou?*'s drug references are rampant, refer to cocaine, among other drugs, and clearly depict a visceral need for their use.

26. Biographical material comes from the following sources: Stanley Frank, "Now I Stash Me Down to Nod," *Esquire* 21 (June 1944): 53, 168–70; Konrad Nowakowski, "Dan Burley—His Career as a Pianist and Writer," in *South Side Shake: 1945–1951,* by Dan Burley, CD, Wolf Records. WBJ 008 CD; Jim Reisler, "Dan Burley: The Most Versatile Black Journalist of His Generation," in *Black Writers/Black Baseball: An Anthology of Articles from Black Sportswriters Who Covered the Negro Leagues* (Jefferson, NC: McFarland, 1994), 127–44; and the obituaries in *Jet,* Nov. 8, 1962, and *New York Amsterdam News,* Nov. 3, 1962.

27. Clarence Major, "Introduction," in *Juba to Jive: A Dictionary of African American Slang* (New York: Penguin Books, 1994), xxvii–xxxv; Harold Wentworth and Stuart Berg Flexner, eds., *Dictionary of American Slang* (New York: TY Crowell, 1967), xi–xii; and James D. Hart, "Jazz Jargon," *American Speech* 7 (April 1932): 241–42.

28. Cons, "The Slanguage of Swing," 1.

29. Lawrence Lipton, *The Holy Barbarians* (New York: Julian Messner, 1959), 38–40.

30. Hurstson's novel was originally published in 1939. For quote on the internality of freedom, see Zora Neale Hurston, *Moses, Man of the Mountain* (New York: Harper Perennial, 1991), 282.

31. The quoted version is actually Hughes's second. He first published the poem in 1931, then again in his 1967 collection *The Panther and the Lash.* For further analysis of "Christ in Alabama," including the fundamental differences between the two versions, see Stanley Schatt, "Langston Hughes: The Minstrel as Artificer," *Journal of Modern Literature* 4 (September 1974): 115–20; and Karen Jackson Ford, "Making Poetry Pay: The Commodification of Langston Hughes," in *Marketing Modernisms: Self-Promotion, Canonization, Rereading,* ed. Kevin J. H. Dettmar and Stephen Watt, 275–96 (Ann Arbor: University of Michigan Press, 1996). Both versions are printed in the above editions.

32. Arthur K. Spears has made the convincing argument that

overwhelming candor is a core constituent aspect of African American Vernacular English, and can be deployed for both positive and negative purposes. "Directness," in and of itself, is not epithet. To understand what he calls the "uncensored mode" of such language, context must first be established. See Arthur K. Spears, "African-American Language Use: Ideology and So-Called Obscenity," in *African American English: Structure, History, and Usage,* ed. Salikoko S. Mufwene, John R. Rickford, Guy Bailey, and John Baugh (New York: Routledge, 1998), 226–50; and Arthur K. Spears, "Directness in the Use of African-American English," *Sociocultural and Historical Contexts of African-American English,* ed. Sonja L. Lanehart (Philadelphia: John Benjamins. 2001), 239–59.

33. For a fuller discussion of the African American lexicon, slang, and the semantics of mass culture, see the following Selected Bibliography.

34. Tapley and Majied died less than a month apart, both in early 2005. "Black Press Cartoonist Melvin Tapley Dies after Long Illness," http://editorialcartoonists.com/news/article.cfm/415/; and Brother Ahmad Muhammad and Sister Aquellah Muhammad, "A Little History on Brother E. Majied," *Muhammad Speaks,* http://www.muhammadspeaks.com/MAJIED.html. For more on Melvin Tapley's syndicated cartoon work, see Tim Jackson, *Salute to Pioneering Artists of Color,* http://www.clstoons.com.

35. Major, "Introduction," xxvii.

SELECTED BIBLIOGRAPHY

Abrahams, Roger D., and John F. Szwed. "Black English: An Essay Review." *American Anthropologist* 77 (June 1975): 329–35.

Allen, Irving Lewis. *The City in Slang: New York Life and Popular Speech.* New York: Oxford University Press, 1993.

Baugh, John. *Beyond Ebonics: Linguistic Pride and Racial Prejudice.* New York: Oxford University Press, 2000.

———. *Black Street Speech: Its History, Structure, and Survival.* Austin: University of Texas Press, 1983.

Brasch, Ila Wales, and Walter Milton Brasch. *A Comprehensive Annotated Bibliography of American Black English.* Baton Rouge: Louisiana State University Press, 1974.

Bunt, Harry C. *Mass Terms and Model-Theoretic Semantics*. Cambridge: Cambridge University Press, 1985.

Calloway, Cab. *Cab Calloway's Hepsters Dictionary*. New York: self-published, 1938.

Claerbaut, David. *Black Jargon in White America*. Grand Rapids, MI: Eerdmans, 1972.

Cons, Carl. "The Slanguage of Swing: Terms the 'Cats' Use." *Down Beat* 2 (November 1935): 1.

Dillard, J. L. *Black English: Its History and Usage in the United States*. New York: Random House, 1972.

———. *Lexicon of Black English*. New York: Seabury Press, 1977.

Gold, Robert S. *A Jazz Lexicon*. New York: Alfred A. Knopf, 1964.

———. *Jazz Talk*. Indianapolis: Bobbs-Merrill, 1975.

———. "The Vernacular of the Jazz World." *American Speech* 32 (December 1957): 271–82.

Hart, James D. "Jazz Jargon." *American Speech* 7 (April 1932): 241–54.

Haskins, James, and Hugh F. Butts. *The Psychology of Black Language*. New York: Barnes and Noble Books, 1973.

Labov, William. *Language in the Inner City: Studies in the Black English Vernacular*. Philadelphia: University of Pennsylvania Press, 1972.

Leonard, Neil. "The Jazzman's Verbal Usage." *Black American Literature Forum* 20 (spring–summer 1986): 151–60.

Levin, Samuel R. *The Semantics of Metaphor*. Baltimore: Johns Hopkins University Press, 1977.

Major, Clarence. *Dictionary of Afro-American Slang*. New York: International Publishers, 1970.

———. *From Juba to Jive: A Dictionary of African American Slang*. New York: Penguin, 1994.

McRae, Rick. "'What Is Hip?' and Other Inquiries in Jazz Slang Lexicography." *Notes* 57 (March 2001): 574–84.

Mencken, H. L. *The American Language: An Inquiry into the Development of English in the United States*. New York: Knopf, 1962.

Mitchell-Kernan, Claudia. *Language Behavior in a Black Urban Community*. Berkeley: Language Behavior Research Laboratory, 1970.

Morgan, Marchyliena. *Language, Discourse and Power in African American Culture*. Cambridge: Cambridge University Press, 2002.

Mufwene, Salikoko, S., John R. Rickford, Guy Bailey, and John Baugh, eds. *African-American English: Structure, History, and Use*. London: Routledge, 1998.

Nye, Russel B. "A Musician's Word List." *American Speech* 12 (February 1937): 45–48.

Partridge, Eric. *A Dictionary of the Underworld, British and American: Being the Vocabularies of Crooks, Criminals, Racketeers, Beggars and Tramps, Convicts, the Commercial Underworld, the Dry Traffic, the White Slave Traffic, Spivs.* London: Routledge and Kegan Paul, 1949.

Shaw, Arnold. "The Vocabulary of Tin-Pan Alley Explained." *Notes* 7 (December 1949): 33–53.

Shelly, Lou. *Hepcats Jive Talk Dictionary.* Derby, CT: TWO Charles, 1945.

Smitherman, Geneva. *Talkin and Testifyin: The Language of Black America.* Detroit: Wayne State University Press, 1977.

Webb, H. Brook. "The Slang of Jazz." *American Speech* 12 (October 1937): 179–84.

Wentworth, Harold, and Stuart Berg Flexner, eds. *Dictionary of American Slang.* New York: T. Y. Crowell, 1967.

Dan Burley's
ORIGINAL HANDBOOK OF
HARLEM

CONTENTS

FOREWORD TO THE ORIGINAL EDITION
Earl Conrad

Apart from the fact that Dan Burley's jive talk often needs interpretation, Dan Burley himself needs interpretation, but I am not going to attempt that Herculean task. I do say that anyone who could interpret Dan could establish the magic link between the Negro and the white worlds; he could show us how and why one world influences the other, why the two are constantly merging in myriad ways. He who interprets Dan Burley could prophesy the language, the thinking and the people of some future America that I know is on the way. I know it is on the way because Dan is a symptom of it. But he and the strange job that he has done on language is more than a mere symptom: it's a live trend, influence, impact. It is no wonder then, as I write this, I hear that hundreds of people, yea thousands, are already seeking out this book even before the news of it has been fairly bruited about.

Recently, in a rather heavy article in a heavy magazine, the Journal of Negro Education (Spring 1944), I had occasion to speak of Dan Burley's work. It was in an article entitled, "The Philology of Negro Dialect."[1] Here, I'll attempt translating that into a jive title myself: "The Inside of Tan Gumbeating." How is it, Dan? What I said then still goes. These were the words:

"Probably the highest expression, even if it sometimes seems a caricatured expression of what the Negro is rightfully doing to the language that was foisted upon him, is to be found in Dan Burley's writings. Here is a true 'native son' of the Negro-American language, or the Negro transformation of the English language. Here is the idiom transmitted and transfused, extracted and distilled, absorbed and reflected. Through Burley's synthesizing machine there passes the 'native' Negro-American language, idiom, dialect and expression emerging as something new and different in spoken English."

Yes, that's what Dan means to the King's English. Take the tall language of Bill Shakespeare as he uttered it in, say, Hamlet, and put it right next to a column by Dan Burley and what have you got? Well, many things—and I'm not trying to compare Dan and Shakespeare in any way, but I am saying this: Both lingoes belong to the English language. They are worlds apart, and yet jive has its roots in English. But jive has principally roots in America. What jive has done is this: It has taken the influences of the United States on language, mingled them freely with traditional English, and given us a new idiom, a new dialect, a new approach to language.

Mind you, I'm not taking any sides here. I'm not saying that jive talk is better, or clearer, or more useful, or anything else than what we might call straightforward spoken English. I'm saying only that it's here, whether you like it or not. This is just reportage: jive has come on the scene, and I'm telling you, and Dan is showing you. Take it or leave it. Argue it, resent it, accept it, do what you will with it. It's here and you know it or you wouldn't be buying a "Handbook of Jive," and Dan knows it or he wouldn't have written it, and I know it or I wouldn't be talking about it.

And now, to get professional for a minute. I'm going to give you a lesson in semantics. Semantics is the science of meanings, the study of language changes, the study of what happens to words, phrases, even ideas under the influence of what people do to them by altering, modifying, or shortening them. This country, as an example, is cluttered up with regional dialects, with peculiar expressions in different parts of the country: the examination of that is semantics. The difference between Brooklynese and the talk of an Ozark mountaineer is a subject for the semantics expert.

Well, when you talk about jive, bring on your semantics.

Dan Burley has something here that ought to make the semanticists dig down underneath the cellar of their libraries.

For I'm sure that Burley's masterly handling of Negro idiom and dialect and colloquial expression gives us an opportunity to watch, under our very eyes, the changing nature of spoken English.

Burley's jive is, to the student of changing language, what the bacteria under a microscope is to a scientist.

I predict that people who make a study of Negro life and the inter-impact of Negro and white on each other will study Dan Burley's present handbook like bacteriologists now study the chemical changes in matter.

For in a real sense Dan's job represents a chemical change on language. Not a change that he has worked up by himself, but rather one that he has seen in embryo on all sides of himself, and he has picked it up, reported it, added to it, polished it. And now you get it in the form of some very fine poetry.

That, as I see it, is the reason why jive is here to stay. It has poetic possibilities in it. Under Dan's handling at least, you get a strange new imagery, one that the poet can see, feel, admire.

I'm not saying that all the expressions that Dan uses in the course of this book are good ones, permanent ones, clear or useful ones. I do say that there's a helluva lot in it that is already permanent idiom in Negro America.

Jive is one more contribution of Negro America to the United States. White America perpetrated a new and foreign language on the Africans it enslaved. Slowly, over the generations, Negro America, living by and large in its own segregated world, with its own thoughts, found its own way of expression, found its own way of handling English, as it had to find its own way in handling many other aspects of a white, hostile world. Jive is one of the end-results. In its present form it may be transitory, subject to more change. I'm sure it will be. But here is an arsenal of it that proves a process has been at work.

I think that jive has some such origin as this: It may go way back, deep into the bowels of the Negro-American experience, back into the revolutionary times when it was necessary for the Negro to speak, sing and even think in a kind of code. We know that the Negro's music grew up out of his revolutionary experience, that his spirituals reflected his struggle, his "escape to the North." Jive talk may have been originally a kind of "pig Latin" that the slaves talked with each other, a code—when they were in the presence of whites. Take the word "ofay." Ninety-million white Americans right now probably don't know that that means "a white," but Negroes know it. Negroes needed to have a word like that in their language, needed to create it in self-defense.

Have you ever walked into a grocery store or a place of business of some sort and heard the proprietor and his wife talk in a foreign language when they didn't want you to hear what they were discussing? Well, the Negro has had a similar way of passing on his thoughts, via jive, to his fellow blacks, when whites were around.

I've sat around Harlem eateries and listened to the talk sometimes—and I'm an old hand at this game, having been around the community a great many years—but occasionally I'll hear brief snatches of talk, curious little expressions, the snatch of a phrase—things I hardly get or don't get. Whites, less initiated than myself, listening to this, wouldn't understand a word they were hearing. It would sound completely alien. I think this tone has something to do with the way jive has come into being.

Dan's jive parodies of famous pieces like "The Night Before Christmas," and other poems will remind some readers of the parodies done by Milt Gross in his series "Nize Boy" in the old World many years ago.[2] Gross's language was English as it was handled with the twist of Yiddish dialect, and it stemmed from the imperfect speech of recent Yiddish immigrants. It, too, had its philological significance. But while that type of dialect is apt to be a temporary thing (the second generation of Jews uses standard English) you will find that jive has a different origin and possibly a different future. Jive, as indicated, is from way back, and it is crystallizing and growing under our eyes, as a native, roots-in-America process. Some of its influence is here to stay, to permanently mark the spoken English of Negro and white.

What jive means, how it has come to be with us, and where and what it might possibly lead to is actually a long story. I wouldn't be surprised if one day soon one of those semantics fellows might come along and do one of those heavy books with footnotes at the bottom of the page and long-winded language, one of those books that'll sell a total of 427 copies. This is not that book and this is not that type of introduction.

Well, let's let Dan carry the ball from here. Give a hand to the first "Handbook of Jive" in America.

PREFACE

This volume is intended as a guide and handbook designed primarily to give students of Jive, and those who would like to be "in the know" on this newest and most popular addition to the modern American dialect, an idea of what it is all about. The author's purpose is to present as clearly as circumstances permit what Jive is; to what use it can be put; and by examples open the way to an adoption of it by the reader, if he be so inclined, to put to whatever use that may be desired. That is why the effort has been put forth to present Jive, both written and spoken, as employed by its actual proponents, even though this form is continually undergoing a process of change, a kind of evolution in which new words and phrases are tried and old ones discarded as obsolete. At the same time, there is an attempt made at classifying and condensing the ever-growing vocabulary and increasing literature of Jive, so that the reader and earnest student may obtain a comprehensive idea of the way Jive is and can be used in every day conversation and correspondence.

The author, recognizing the curiosity with which the average reader will pick up this book, has made a somewhat radical step in arranging the contents. It was felt that the number one consideration was to satisfy those who are curiously interested in Jive and not necessarily worried or concerned with the etymology, syntax, and the social background of this form of slang. With that view in mind, what etymology, syntax and social background of Jive there is has been placed in the back of the book and the reader is then introduced immediately to the subject in the first chapters. It will be found that this arrangement even puts the lexicon or dictionary of Jive phrases and words ahead of the "heavier" and more "solid" aspects of Jive. But the alleged sacrifice is believed justified when the inclinations of the average reader are taken into consideration. Thus, those who are reading purely for entertainment and diversion will not be weighed down with a lot of formal explanation, abstract discussion, and so forth, just at the place where one would rather not be bothered.

The author wishes to thank Langston Hughes, the celebrated Negro poet, to whom he is deeply indebted for this effort, because it was Mr. Hughes who insisted that such a book be written by the author. He felt that Jive was developing and attracting so much attention that the writer, as one of the pioneer exponents of slang, usually credited with originating most of the phrases and words in popular use, should be the one to write a book on the subject, containing examples based on material which have appeared from time to time in his column, "Back Door Stuff," a feature in the *New York Amsterdam News*, leading Negro weekly newspaper, of which the author is the managing editor. To Drs. C. B. Powell and P. M. H. Savory, co-publishers and editor and treasurer respectively of the *New York Amsterdam News*, the writer tenders thanks for their kind permission to reprint material used in their newspaper and for the encouragement he has received from them in gathering material for the book. The writer is also indebted to many others, including George Davis, associate editor of the magazine *Mademoiselle*; to Earl Wilson, nightclub editor of the *New York Post*; to Haskell Cohen, free-lance writer and journalist; to Stanley Frank, war correspondent and famous sports columnist on the *New York Post*; to Harry Markson of the Twentieth Century Sporting Club; to Stanley Woodward, sports editor of the *New York Herald Tribune*; to Miss Eleanor Parker who typed and revised the original manuscript; to Dan Parker, militant sports editor of the *New York Daily Mirror*; to A. M. Wendell Malliet, Harlem's only Negro book publisher[3]; to Miss Blanche Lawyer, my able secretary; to Melvin Tapley, whose clever, original drawings illustrate this book; to Dr. Frederick D. Carter, widely known young Harlem chiropodist–actor who, when I was trying to make readers of my column and others Jive-conscious, volunteered to learn and recite poetic pieces and other bits at the various functions where he was billed to perform; to John Johnson, editor of the magazine, *Negro Digest*[4]; to Earl Conrad, author of "Harriet Tubman" and New York newspaperman; and particularly to my loyal, devoted wife, Gustava McCurdy, for the encouragement, patient, unselfish belief in this effort, without which little would have been done. In passing, the author would also like to thank the thousands and thousands of soldiers, sailors, airmen, and others in the Armed Forces, plus the thousands of civilians who have written him letters praising his work on Jive and otherwise encouraging him to write this book.

Dan Burley
New York City
November, 1944

Dan Burley's Original

Handbook of Harlem Jive

1. What Is Jive?

Jive is language in motion. It supplies the answer to the hunger for the unusual, the exotic and the picturesque in speech. It is a medium of escape, a safety valve for people pressed against the wall for centuries, deprived of the advantages of complete social, economic, moral and intellectual freedom. It is an inarticulate protest of a people given half a loaf of bread and then dared to eat it; a people continually fooled and bewildered by the mirage of a better and fuller life. Jive is a defense mechanism, a method of deriving pleasure from something the uninitiated cannot understand. It is the same means of escape that brought into being the spirituals as sung by American slaves; the blues songs of protest that bubble in the breasts of black men and women believed by their fellow white countrymen to have been born to be menials, to be wards of a nation, even though they are tagged with a whimsical designation as belonging to the body politic. Jive provides a medium of expression universal in its appeal. Its terms have quality, sturdiness, rhythm and descriptive impact. It is language made vivid, vital and dynamic.

Jive serves a definite need of the people the same as do the Knights of Pythias, the Elks, or the Sons and Daughters of I Do Arise, with their signs, passwords, handclasps, and so on. Conversations can be held in Jive to the complete befuddlement of the fellow who doesn't know its meaning. Letters can be composed and written in Jive that will puzzle censors and all others who don't know what it is all about. Jive is a lot of fun.

1. Jive for Jivers and Those Who Are Not

Two hepcats, their hair heavily larded, are standing near the juke box in the candy store. The first hepcat is telling his friend a story. He says:

"Ole man, it's about a tray of haircuts on the backbeat when I nixes my pad, drops my twister on the keep, and collars a light broom down the cruncher to the lushpad on the three pointer. I'm stiffing the stroll on the flag spot when up pops a fine banana with a cluck stud hanging on her crook. I digs the play and rolls it over in my conk that this is a wild banter that's trying to flop but can't fly. Now the cluck stud is in there, ole man, he's in there. He's draped out in a cutting blue with rolls as big as a needle's eye, and spreading like the mumps at his deuce of benders. His sky is righteous and hooks over his gimmers like pie crust over the rim of a pan. His treaders, ole man, are brand new and his tops hit him across his ticker with the straps as short as my cash. That fine banana, ole man, understand, is as mellow as a cello; as fine as red wine; a killer from Manila; like the tree, ole man, understand?, all root. Like the bear's brother Eddie, Jack, she's ready. She's righteous, ole man; she's reacheous and she's shaped up like a Coca-Cola bottle, wide open at the throttle. In fact, stud hoss, she's as pretty as a speckled pup climbing a green hill under a country wagon on a summer afternoon in June. She's in her dried barkers like kong in glassware, and those gams, ole man, understand, are like the props on a goola. My conk said grey, but Jackson, I dug the sniffer, a button, ole man, understand? That gave her away.

"I want to lay my larceny, but the cluck's done cruised her through the slammer before I can shift to second. But I cops a drill right after them, ole man, and I dug my broom, quite racy, like Count Basie. Inside they're spraying with their cutware upside down, and I digs that all the stud's laying down is a deuce of demons, because he don't spread nothing but thins on the line. At the same time, homey, I'm eating onions and wiping my eyes: just like the chicken, I ain't sticking. Yet, all the time, I'm rolling it in my conk that he's a Lane from Spokane, or at most, a Home from Rome. I'm figuring what's the jive and how I'm gonna cut in, when the stud cuts out to drop a flat in the piccolo. While he's wriggling and twisting with the pic, I'm gunning this fine banana, and she finally gims me kinda hard, ole man, just like Norwegian lard. I hooks and she latches on, because I digs him two camels down the road doing a solo in a boulevard westerner as though he was in a hurry to get back.

"Ole man, I tunes my brace of receivers in real sharp and eases around until I'm right by this fine banana. Here's the spiel I laid on her:

"Listen, Babes, you're mellow, understand? I dug you when you popped in port. You're making the wrong play; I'm your light of day. That square ain't nowhere. I'm the accelerator; you're the moderator, ain't you got no pressure to spare? I can make you mellow, but you gotta nix out that fellow. I'm a hipped cat, understand?"

"Now here's what she laid on me:

"'I believe, my friend, your name is West; you're working hard to bust your vest. Sure, I'm mellow and I'm a solid frail; you've got the right hammer but you use the wrong nail. You're picking up nickels and laying down dimes, but your jive is beat and sour as limes'."

The lowdown on this report by the hepcat can be picked up through study of the lexicon, called the "Jiver's Bible," in the back of this book.[5] However, to start the reader off, the author felt some explanation was necessary. Here is what was said: "My friend, about three weeks ago I left home, gave my key to the housekeeper, and walked down the avenue to the tavern on the corner. I'm standing there where the bus stops, loafing, when a pretty yellow girl comes along with a very dark individual holding her arm. I look them over quickly and decide that she is a gay young woman who is out for fun in the nightlife whirl for the first time. Now her companion is flashily dressed in the latest style. He is wearing a sharply pressed blue suit, the trousers of which are very small at the ankles, and very large and balloon-like at the knees. He has on a good hat, the brim of which is turned down over his eyes in the latest Harlem fashion. His shoes are brand new. The tops of his trousers are so high they reach his heart. His suspenders are as short as can be. That fine high yellow girl is easy to look at; in fact, she's everything a man would want in a woman. She fits into her furs like whiskey in a bottle. Her legs are shapely and rounded as the legs on a piano. At first I thought she was a white girl, but when I observed her nose, it was as flat as a button. I, thus, found she was colored. You see, I wanted to get in a word with her, but her companion rushed her through the door before I could move. I walked in behind them casually. Inside, they were drinking, and I saw at once that her escort was spending only a few dimes. At the same time, my friend, I realize that I haven't any money; in fact, I'm dead broke. Yet, all the time, I'm thinking her companion is just a nice fellow, or at most, a working man. I'm trying to see my way clear to horn in on them when he gets up to drop a nickel in the music box. While he is busy with the juke box, I'm staring at her. She finally looks at me. I nod to her and she seems to understand because I see her boy friend fifteen minutes later riding in a taxicab as though he were anxious to be gone and get back. I listen closely to everything she says and move to her side. I tell her she is lovely and that I saw her when she entered the place. I tell her she is out with the wrong person; that I am the type of man she should be with, and that her friend doesn't mean a thing to her. I also tell her that I am the kind of man with whom she would find enjoyment being out with. I ask if she will share her affections with me. I further tell her that I can show her a pleasant evening but that she will have to leave her friend. Here's what she told me:

"'I believe, my friend, that you are a most unusual person, but you're working overtime to get yourself in trouble. Sure, I'm a good looking girl, and you've got a good line of talk, but not for me. You think yourself very charming and clever, but your story is weak; in fact, it leaves me cold, and doesn't sound good at all'."

2. Putting Down a Righteous Spiel

(This bit of conversation between Sam D. Home and Joe Q. Hipp, Harlem's mythical topflight spielers of jive, could have been recorded on the corner of 126th Street and Seventh Avenue, where, it seems, most of the good jive conversations are held.)

"Ole man, whatcha putting down?" asked Sam D. Home as his friend, Joe Q. Hipp sauntered up. "I'm picking up on everything brown; ole man, what are you putting down?"

"Pops, I'm tops," replied Joe Hipp, "I'm with it, and I won't quit it. I'm down with the action to my own satisfaction. Do you dig?"

"I'm suffering with the shorts, because all of the reports, make the future dims and brights unhipped on the blacks and whites, so I'm stashing my play right here," said Sam D. Home.

"Let me boot you to my play and, maybe, you can pick up on the issue I put down with this action," declared Joe Q. Hipp. "I dug a skull a deuce of haircuts on the backbeat of the trey thirty putting down a spiel on a heavy hen on the main trill in front of the lush stash on the three pointer."

"What was the skull laying, ole man? What was he putting down?"

"Well, the skull was coming on like I've Just Gone with a beg act on the hen's glory roll. He was jiving and conniving, ole man, with an issue that I used to knock out when I was putting down some lemon pool action with the smooth roundies when doing a paper dolly at the knowledge stash in the days when I was a cool fool knocking my trill to the swimming pool, trying to beat out the play on the golden rule."

"That's mad, ole man; so mad it's glad," commented Sam D. Home. "Keep a spieling."

"Well, the skull was spreading his propaganda that he'd been scoffing on fishheads and scrambling for the gills until this heavy hen tracked down the mid. He was knocking her down to his stash in life and, ole man, he was putting the jive on her that she was the mellow, yellow wren, the angel of all forgotten men; and how it was her duty, like good tutti-fruitti, to come up on some beater to straighten out his condition."

"I digs that beg act, poppa," said Sam D. Home. "I'm hard with a play like that myself, although it's as old as ice is cold. Keep a beefing."

"Well," continued Joe Q. Hipp, "the heavy hen was all for the issue, and was getting ready to lay down a few dead ones on this skull, when up pops a banter play built on a coke frame, frocked down to ain't it a shame, with some good-doing moss without the unhipped gloss, and put her wing in his, and started dropping a hype of her own."

"That's the way they'll do, ole man. These chicks will come down on an issue every time. What did the banter take off with?"

"Well, here's her beef; she says, 'Pops, I just fell in from the Big Wind; I've been on a tab issue for many a dim and bright, and I'm beat for the yolk, and dying to meet some folk who'll be with it on the knock play. I've been gimming every play along the line, ole man, for the stud that put me down after he'd jived me into laying a broom to that repent pad. I had a mellow slave knocking off hen tracks on a rolltop piano, and I wasn't booted to the inside plays that come up on the turf'."

"That's some mellow mess, Joe; just like 'Porgy and Bess.' You're putting down a gasser, poppa-stoppa; that's a gasser from back."

"The chick tells how she was knocking her dead ones on the nose each and every double trey; and how the issue is mellow and the action fine and how her rolltop piano hen tracks are solid with the head kick, and how she went to knock a scoff one mid-bright and how a skull pops up beside her and laid a hype on her."

"What did the skull drop on her?" Sam D. Home asked. "I've dug a lot of hypes, but this one is like my Aunt Bessie— fine and groovy and kinda messy. Spiel on, my man, spiel on."

"The skull, according to her beef, said: 'Babes, you're too mellow 'n' yellow to come up on that slave tip. The righteous riff to put down is to let me call the plays and you dig the ways. I'm hipped to my deuce of benders; I'm called by every cat and stud in the land, the righteous, the solid Mister Man! I'm above the issue like an ocean gull; that's why, Babes, the boys call me Skull'."

"Solid, ole man, solid," breathed Sam D. Home in admiration. "I'm gonna hen track that issue. It's mad and really ready for my pad."

"Well, the banter went for the issue, and snipped a paper dolly at the rolltop piano, and went to stash in the skull's walk-back on the topside of the rockpile on the heavy lump. The banter used to dig a tube when she trumped the lump and the skull, for a while, kept his word, and she didn't have to put down on the Before Abe Jive. But shortly after, the skull came up on the tab action, and gassed the scribe that he was beat for some beater, and wanted her to weed him a holler note until his mudder came in."

"Jeez, Jake, that's a low snake; that stud was putting down a hard hype. I likes hard hypes like that; I'm a hyper who blows like a piper myself. What else?"

"The banter had been spinning at the track on fool's dim, and she was ready as Mister Freddy on all the riffs and rills that come on the short trills. So, the skull had been laying a scoff on her so long and letting her collar her nod on a zoom for so long, she couldn't quit it as long as she was with it. She latched onto a Lane from Fort Wayne, and let him down for his chimer, but the Lane was booted to that onion action, and came up with a kill joy, who tagged the play with the slammer issue, but the skull sniffed a powder.

"When the banter got through spieling, ole man, the heavy hen was ready to dust, but the banter laid her stealers on her flappers and booted her to the jive that the skull was trying to drop a hype on her like the one he had put down too long before. Now the skull was draped in bull's wool, and the banter knew the play. She flagged a kill joy who soon had Mister Speaker facing the skull. And that's that."

"You mean the skull stumbled and fell, tripping up in the threads he had picked up on?" asked Sam D. Home in sober amazement.

"That's with it, ole man," rejoined Joe Q. Hipp. "That's with it. You dug it like I rug it. I'm knocking my trill. Dig you."

3. Jive Points and Viewpoints

They talk about everything in jive. The hepcat and flychick on the corner, in the candy store, in the school locker rooms, in the theatre lobby, use jive as a medium to discuss mutual problems, to get "loads off their chests," secure in the assumption that what they are saying isn't being understood by the wrong pair of ears. Although jive originated among Negroes, it has no color line. In fact, jive has broken down quite a few barriers of race itself. The conversation recorded here is an indication of the trend of thinking prevalent among young folks today.

Two cats, one white, the other colored, were stashed on the flag spot on the three pointer of the ace trill in the twirling top one righteous cool, laying down their larceny on all issues, including hype-dropping, and pick-ups and put-downs. The colored cat was on the beam, and here's part of his spiel—

"Ole man, I've been digging the snitches each and every bright and dim, and daddy, the action that is going on is heavy on all fronts; and those who ain't hipped better get their boots on, 'cause there's a lot of shuck dropping going on, and there's a lotta heads that are going to be oiled up before this mess is straightened out."

"I dig you, stud hoss," cut in the white cat. "I'm with the issue and down with the action, especially since it's built on a solid half-traction. The grey issue on the cornpone side of the black and white split is putting down a play that isn't hipped at all. They don't dig that this is 1944, and not 1844. Homes don't come from Rome no more. Neither do all Lanes come from Spain and Squares from Delaware. There's too many hipped spades mixed up in this issue to take all that wringling and twisting on their knees."

"Ole man," said the colored cat, "You're groovy as a ten cent movie with that line. In fact, it's fine. I like your patter; it's right over the platter. What those grey studs on the unglamorous side of the cornpone riff don't cop is that the average Lane today is from the Apple, or at least from some Apple, whether it's the Big Apple, the Windy Apple, the Tropic Apple, or the Bunker Hill Apple, and he's down with the action since he ain't never had to get bouncy in his brace of duke's because a grey wouldn't play the game like it should be played. These young studs are oilers from back, and pops, they're shooting their marbles from all sides of the ring. Since Uncle laid down his play and put the issue on them, these cats are too hipped to sit down when they should stand up."

"That zoot suit action," said the white cat, "wasn't hipped. In fact, it was sorry off-jiving. Where do them studs get off trying to call a riff like that? A play where the issue is that we can't knock our drapes and righteous shapes the way we want 'em? I still say this is 1944. Cats have changed, ole man, and they don't come through the back like they used to.

"Us young homes, and lanes and hipstuds, grey and fay, and spook and spade, are getting together on what's in life, and that's what's got everybody all stewed up. They can't dig a spade and a fine young grey scribe copping a tapper on the main drag. Neither can they latch onto the issue on which a young grey cat will help a spook oil up another grey who doesn't know this is 1944."

"And Jackson," added the white cat, "Uncle is hipping a whole lot of cats as to what to do when the action gets off the track. And he's knocking the info to each of these cats as how to take charge when the mess gets too thick to thin out. A lotta greys and some ungroovy spooks, for that matter, are going to get conked up good before everybody sits down and cops a scoff from the same oak spread. I hope you dig me, ole man, 'cause I dig you."

Thus, it can be seen that crude social implications are prevalent in many jive conversation and "modern ideas" present in many breasts of those who speak and think in jive. The intermingling of white and Negro youth has brought about a degree of intimacy that would have been unthinkable in another era. With jive they feel safe. It is a medium that allows them full expression, and at the same time, provides the diversion fads and fancies jive is supposed to provide.

JOHN GREENLEAF WHITTIER'S

"THE BAREFOOT BOY"

A Parody in Harlem Jive

> Blessings on Thee, Little Square,
> Barefoot Cat with the unconked hair;
> With thy righteous pegtop pants,
> And thy solid hepcat's stance,
> With thy chops so red and mellow,
> Kissed by chicks so fine and yellow;
> With the bean beaming on thy crown,
> That sky of thine such a bringdown;
> My own tick-tock to thee I bare,
> I was once an unhipped Square,
> A Lane, thou art; Poppa Stoppa
> Is only a pigeon dropper!
> Let the Cats with gold go trotting,
> Barefoot, knock thy trill while plotting,
> Thou has more than Cat can lam—

In the reach of gim and gam;
Outward foxy, inward, mop!
Blessings on thee, Junior Hop.
Oh, for Homey's righteous fun,
The nod that's hip as "two and one";
Jack, you can dig the bagman's play,
Solidly in there, all the way;
Of the buzzer's frantic flight,
Of the sweet-smell's glamour bright;
Trill of flippers to their crib,
Of Frank Buck's most fine contrib;
How the stiffback packs his frame;
How the digger ducks from blame;
How the cruncher digs his fame;
How the chirper knocks a scoff;
How the flit-flit's pad is soft;
Where the ofay sweet-smells stash;
And where the groovy red ones splash;
Where the jaw-breaker brooms along,
Where the kong-maker's vines belong;
Of the spade stinger's knowledge box,
Building his pad with tiny rocks;
The cooking up of real hip plays,
The Head Knock collars all he lays;
Skin in skin with her he steals,
Pan to pan with her he spiels;
Thus you dig this righteous pair,
Blessings on thee, Little Square.

Oh, for the sweat stretch of the year,
Stashing the twelves in one short beer;
When all the Jive I copped or dug,
Me, the Head Knock, was really drug;

I was in there, ole man, sweet-smells and twigs;
Baby, chirps, and buzzing gigs;
Had my fun, the nut-scoffer jumped;
The cruncher was solidly humped;
That scoff of blackberries most fine,
Right and mellow, good doin' wine!
The brook, ole man, was also hip,
And through the bright and dim that trip,
Spieling at the garden wall,
Gum-beating with me, treetop tall!
Mine, the jaw-breaker layout there,
In the orchard, Home, not like the Bear:
The one per day so finely hung,
I could hardly be so young;
My dead Presidents piled most high,
All the Apple I dug so fly,
A frantic, anxious, mighty dome,
Blessings on thee, little home,
Barefoot Square, Just Here from Rome.

Oh, for a scoff, laid out so fine,
Like my cutware with milk, 'tis mine;
A super-scooper, Jackson, Boy,
On the slammer's chimer, floy-floy;
O'er me like the Head Knock's crib,
Dig them splashes; sharp as my chib;
All jived up as Hawkins blows,
While the grunter blows his nose.
Nothing in the one per day,
That could boot me, so to say;
Makes no difference what you wear;
Blessings on thee, Little Square,
Barefoot Cat with the unconked hair.

THE NIGHT BEFORE XMAS

'Twas the dim before Nicktide, and all through the Crib,
You could hear Joe Hipp spieling that righteous ad lib.
Them leg-sacks were stashed by the smoke-hole, in fact,
They were a Lamb's unhipped beg on Santa's fine sack;
The cats and the chippies were all knocking a nod,
While the most anxious ideas through their thinkboxes trod;
And the Head Chick was snorting, but I tossed and rolled,
Trying to collar a wink, as Hawkins blew cold;
"Let your gimmers pop open," loudly cried Joe Hipp,
I bounced from my softy, gave the lilies a flip,
Trillied to the glass-gazer to dig the outside;
And in the heavy pitch black, overhead I spied,
The pumpkin riding gently, and grinning so fine,
It was digging its kicks from the gleaming snow-shine;
The gazers were packed with Lamb, Chippie and Square,
Including Fuzzy-Wuzzy, and Madam St. Clair;
Among them you could dig those with their boots unlaced,
And those who wore them to the armpits tightly braced;
The solid ones, all hipped to the most righteous Jive,
And those drags who were bringdowns, the last to arrive;

At a gazer alone, up near the Mighty Dome,
Squatted your boy, and my boy, Samuel D. Home,
While at another gazer, two floors beneath,
Was the Black Venus peeking from behind a wreath;
With a book under her arm, all about Life and Men,
At a fine cellar gazer was the Little Grey Hen;
While at the kitchen slammer, he kept mighty mum,
Was the one you and I know as The Perfect Rum;
Now, Cholly-Hoss, be solid, don't giggle too soon,
For I'm laying this spiel 'bout December in June,
When everybody swore, they couldn't be swayed,
That the St. Nicholas Jive wouldn't make the grade.
Now, I've never been 'lit up' and righteously high;
When my boots were not on, and my thinkbox not spry.
I'm spieling about something, it ain't hard to guess,
You'll swear it's a gasser, how about that mess?
I dug a slider, ole man, way up in the sky.
And you'll never dig what it was pulled by:
Four deuces of groovy trotters; the biggest of sleds;
All mellow and racy from their hoofs to their heads;
Now please dig this Jive closely, in fact, read it twice,
Because it's finer, Stud Hoss, than fatback and rice;
Them trotters were brooming, and laying their drive,
Right over our crib, and Jack, that's no weedheaded Jive;
And 'twas then that I dug the Stud cracking the whip,
He was solid and fine, like he'd just left his ship;
His drape was more mellow than you'd ever believe,
He was in it, Cholly Hoss, from collar to sleeve.
It glowed like a weed so fine 'n' red in the dark,
As the vipers lighted up by passing the spark.
That coat really cut his frame, just fit him enough,
And the shoulders were padded; Jack, dig that cuff!

29

And his boots came up over his fat benders two,
While, from his double-bumper, a long, white mop grew;
He had his brace o' grabbers in some gloves, coffee-black,
And them trotters were cutting at every whip crack;
We all were knocked out by that Stud's classy lid,
As the trotters, and the slider, on our roof slid;
And that skypiece was curling, like a funnel, old man,
As Mister Hawkins flapped it round like a hothouse fan;
He began some whistling and shouting out loud.
Laid a spiel on his nags that had just rode the cloud;
"Now, Dasher! Now, Dancer! Now, Prancer and Vixen!
On, Comet! On, Cupid! Not a stride we're nixin'!
To the top of the fresh air parlor, dig that wall!
Now cop a trot. Cop a trot! Then cop a squat, all!"

I'm not so sure, but ole man, I'll have to presume,
This is above your knowledge, like Paris perfume;
However, I must, to my spiel again return,
That of this frantic occurrence, more you may learn;
With his slide loaded down with all righteous things,
The strange Stud popped out, as though he wore two wings;
We all ducked away from the glass gazers bright,
As we heard the stud fall down the smoke-hole that night;

"Cheese 'n' crackers, Jack!" shouted Samuel D. Home,
"Guess I'd be better off, if I were back in Rome."
In a voice just a whisper, I dug Madam St. Clair,
Saying, "I guess I'll start looking for Big Jack, The Bear."
Black Venus was quiet, like the Little Grey Hen,
While Fuzzy-Wuzzy watched the chiming Big-Ben;
The Head Chick had long since nixed from her mellow pad,
And was humming a tune about, "I Got It Bad."

From attic to basement, we all knocked a stroll
To the parlor, in time to lamp the old smoke-hole;
The soot that came out, ole man, was heavy and black,
And behind it there slid the Stud, sharp as a tack;
But, instead of that color, most righteous of Red,
The Stud had gone midnight from his feet to his head;
And the bag on his shoulders was bulgingly fat,
With playthings and presents for each chippie and cat;
There were packages of tea—the most righteous tea,
And the vipers all shouted and clapped loud with glee;
There were drapes and togs and skypieces all truly fine,
And lots of bottles and jugs, 'twas mostly all wine;
The drapes were cut straight, ole man, were really most mad,
And would fit your fine brown frame, however, you were clad;
The old Stud had the goodies, Jackson, what a scarf,
'Twould have made a giant out of the smallest dwarf;
Red beans and rice, and finest of ole avenue tripe,
Please believe me, Cholly Hoss, I'm laying no hype.

He loosened up his big bag, dumped out all the things,
And we all started scrambling grabbing everything,
In the mad, unhipped scuffling, and fighting for gifts,
Joe Hipp started in whistling some groovy, fine riffs;
And the Little Brown Banter, as each one should know,
Was all hipped and quite ready, she spun the piccolo;
The cats grabbed the chippies, and St. Nick forgot,
And began some rug cutting, to music most hot,
St. Nicholas was so angry, he became a drag,
And grabbed up the fine presents, putting them in his bag,
He whistled to his trotters, the four deuces of steeds,
And the ole Stud brought me down by grabbing the weeds;
Then he copped a quick trot to the smoke-hole once more,
As the Cats and the Chippies cut rug to the floor;

In a flash he was gone, and all that was left,
Was a bottle of red wine, fruit of Joe Hipp's theft;
Now, believe me, Cholly Hoss, I tell you no lie,
And I'll stick by my story 'till the day I die,
With my deuce of fine peekers, I dug ole St. Nick,
And I'm swearing 'twas him, and it wasn't a trick;
We have talked of it often, just among the crowd,
How the Stud copped a trot once again to the cloud;
He left us no evidence to prove I'm not lying—
But how about Joe Hipp, and that bottle of wine?

The Soliloquy from Shakespeare's "Hamlet" in Harlem Jive

A Parody

To Dig, or not to Dig, Jack, that's the Question;
Whether 'tis the proper play to eat Onions
And wipe the eyes, while laying down one's deepest Jive;
Or to snap open one's fine switch, turn out the joint,
Making cats take low, by much head cutting:
To nix out for good, or to cop a nod no more,
Is solid chow for heartache and a solid grand,
O' heebie-jeebies this body o'mine,
Fine, brown 'n' mellow, collared at birth.
'Tis a weedhead's dream to cop a plea, Aye,
To pass out, or to knock off a brace o'
Nods, mayhaps, dig my kicks as that Cat,
Morpheus, sends me right out of this world:
But, Jack, that's where the play brings me down,
For, if I'm layin' that no-wake nod, the Jive

Ol' Morph may shoot under my fine gims might
Knock me out, so that I might seem a Square,
Like the Bear, Jack, laying his spiel at the Worldly Fair,
And Man, you gotta dig the real Jive, that
Suffering with the shorts is like the spiel
My Chippie lays down, like the kong that
Runs in rivers in the gage joints on the Stem;
For what cat can collar the slave o' whips
An' loud and long spieling by some unhipp'd,
Unglamorous lane who tries a pressure
Play, when the lovebug freezes in the summer weather,
When the "boys in blue" kick the gong around while
The "Homies" in the King's Row show off their backsides,
And the gate that 'easy-does-it' plugging
Of some unhipp'd Square gets; when he, himself,
Might make things mellow with a keen-edge chib?
Who would Sinbad, the Sailor, play, man,
And beatin' up the gums, living the life,
Rocked to the socks by Ole Man Mose, who
Can't get back from the Jersey Side, burns me,
Hoss, and makes me figure 'tis the proper play to
Lay low, right here, than to broom down to some
Square, who might not latch on to righteous Jive.
Thus, the think-pad makes homeboys of us all
And as ol' Shakespeare dug, sco's 'n' blows ago,
The solid yeller of a cat's cooked up play,
Stinks like a corny trumpet with the ofay
Arrangement of the conkpiece, and like the
Rooster, the killer-diller Jive gets screwy
And don't pour just like it used to.
How 'boot this heavy mess, ole man?
How boot it?

LEGEND OF THE SEVEN SKULLS

"Ole man, pull in and cop a squat on a soft one, and latch onto this hype I'm dropping, about the spiel that was laid on the Seven Skulls.

"Now a Lane from Spokane met the Home from Rome, who dug the Square from Delaware hunting Madame St. Clair with the conk in her hair. And Fuzzy-Wuzzy, the Hep Little Huzzy, was seeking her Fame with Ain't It A Shame; and the jive started off from there. They all got together in some unrighteous weather; and beat their gums about the Brooklyn Bums, and the dolls some cats call Gulls.

"Now several of these birds were exchanging words, about hipcats who are booted to the play; about vipers and studs in frantic duds; and foxy chicks, togged to the bricks. They were gathered, these Gulls, about a fire, and laying it down quite mellow; when one with a smile (the beautiful child) said, "Listen to my spiel: It was a deuce of dims and brights ago, in a crib up on the hill, that I dug Seven Skulls with just one roach, gently copping their trill. Now all were tall, each one six feet; they were hipped to the Jive, I swear. They tabled all begs, all reet, all reet, and made things bad for a Square. They knocked a stash in a slammer quite wide, and passed the spark around. And each was solid with his parachute, mellow and ready to glide.

"Seven times the roach crawled around, it got shorter on its many trips. Until the spark could barely been seen as the Skulls put it to their lips. The air got hot (and the gage was right), as the Skulls kept blasting away. And the weed got good (it was round and white) and the Skulls decided to play.

"'I want a chippie just from Mississippi,' shouted Skull Number One.

"'And I want a Chick built up like a brick,' Number Two said when One was done.

"'Give me a hen who wants to sin,' declared Skull Number Three. A silence ensued, and it mellowed the mood, as the four tried to agree.

"Then Number Four said, 'Dress mine in red, with plenty of rear action drive.'

"With the roach in his mouth (he was from the far South), then spieled my Boy Number Five: 'I dig all plays, and plant all lays, Ole Man, that ain't no jive; I want my banter to really canter, she must be five by five.'

"'I'm death on Hicks,' said Number Six, 'The chick I want is yellow; like Norwegian lard, she's gotta be hard, righteous, fine and mellow.'

"The roach was fading, its flame nearly gone, the dim was almost black, when Number Seven pops his chops, and laid this shot on the rack:

"'For me,' said he, 'Give me my bread, and sure as I'm a Skull, I want one bright, and damned near white, fine as an Ocean Gull.'"

36

Now I hope you're hepped
And haven't slept
Through this mad and booted Hype;
'Cause it's in the groove,
(And it's bound to move)
Like righteous avenoo tripe;
Now if you ain't hip,
Better button up your lip;
And call a spade a spade;
Pull up your sox,
Comb your knowledge box,
And slip the Nip a drip!

A Home Boy's Dream

Now Homey was a Home Boy, a strictly Hometown Square;
He never went to dances unless "mama" was right there.
He went to bed at seven, was fast asleep at nine,
While other cats were drinking Harlem's mellow, blood-red wine;
His shoe soles never needed mending, (he cut no rug, you see);
And his life was unoffending since he craved no company.
But Homey couldn't collar just what in life he'd missed;
(Though oftentime he'd wonder 'bout the chicks he'd never kissed).
To bed he went one evening, as the rain came gently down,
While the hot spots were a-jumping all over Harlemtown.
He closed his eyes quite tightly in slumber sweet and long,
And his breathing sounded gently to the sandman's dreamy song:
'Twas after he had settled for his usual nightly snooze,
That he started in a dreaming of the Cat That Never Mews.
The Cat came up and shook him, rather rough, 'tis understood,
And the Homey was quite frightened; it didn't do him any good.
The Cat was togged out mellow, ready in a cuttin' blue,
And his cuffs were tight as funnels, his knees were baggy, too;
He wore a mellow skypiece, a drape that hit him square
Across the hips, real solid, like the Bear, he was somewhere!
His shoes were solid leather, they fitted him just right;

His tops were really righteous, his boots were laced-up tight.
He laid his gims on Homey and dug him up and down,
Then he started in to spieling in jive from Harlemtown;
"You think that you are happy (a Home Boy's idle dream);
'Cause you can't dig what I'm spieling, though it's not what it
    would seem.
They don't pay off on Homeys, they don't pay off on Lanes;
Tighten up your boots, boy, come inside when it rains.
You've got to play the chippies, dig a chick or two;
Stop eatin' ice-cream sundaes, and 'collar' jive that's new.
Discard those togs you're wearing; and knock a drape that's fine;
Get Dan Burley's 'Book for Jivers' and dig yourself a line!
The Apple's slowly twisting, ole man, it really turns;
And you needn't study physics to know that paper burns.
The Cats are eating onions, and their eyes they gently wipe;
For the ruffles are losing favor to that fine ole avenoo tripe;
Uncle is a callin' Homey—Homey and Lane alike;
And he's pitching to the batter, and he doesn't miss a strike;
We Cats are few in number, and you are our new recruit;
We'll teach you how to latch on to jive that really is all-root.
We've got you lined up mellow, with a fine young hen that's
    brown;
Who surely will know how to dig the spiels that you lay down.
Now Homey, forget your mama, forget your papa, too;
And 'boogie' with real feeling in 'a room where lights are blue.'
And when your step grows slower, and your moss turns white
    with care;
Remember you weren't a Homey; you were just a 'perfect Square'."
Then Homey's eyes popped open; in fact they opened wide;
But the Cat had dug a duster, like a Coney Island slide;
So Homey sat and wondered, his thoughts conflicted so;
Whether he would still be Homey, or be known as Jiving Jo?
And if you were our Homey, and had dreamed the same as he,
Would you always be contented a Homey just to be?

"Back Door Stuff"

Dan Burley's Letter to His Column

I dig that you're a solid Cat, and know each and every answer. And I'm hipped that you play the game, three ways sides and flats, and straight across the board. But, Jackson, you're flippin', and you ain't flappin'; you're floppin' and you ain't flyin' a-tall! Ole man, you're still wearing low quarters while I'm stashing my stomps in a fine pair of knee-boots with laces long enough to tie up the Bear's Nephew, Joe, who really doesn't know! In other words, I'm collaring a play that's righteous; really reecheous, in fact, it's roacheous. And, Cholly Hoss, I know just how to slice all corners. Now I'm not playing you 14th Street, but you've gotta go to school, or either dig the heavy spiel these snitchpads are spreading, if you wanna play the game the way I do.

You're slicing your chops about these fine young hens tipping down the crunching straight in the cool of the evening. But, ole man, you're really nowhere with that larceny you're laying, because if you were up on the stickers, like I am, you'd dig that they, themselves, are just out there mugging, hoping that some Cat, without his boots, might broom by, and knock 'em to some fine dried barkers, or at least a scarf that won't choke 'em, or a glass with a little head on.

Back Door Stuff, I've been weeping bitter brine because I thought you had me in Siberia on the Jive that is all-root, but now I dig that you're shooting for the side pocket, and scratching every shot.

There's only three things that count with the cats who play: duck Uncle; dig a righteous pad, and a scarf-ring, trilly 'round the chimer; and latch on to a mellow, young hen with feathers on her wings. Knowing you to be a solemn drag when it comes to digging, and that you might call the cops if the lights turn blue, I'm gonna get you hipped to the spiel I laid down:

In the first place, you know what a solid Cat is, especially if he knows each and every answer, but when you play the game, three ways sides and flats and straight across the board, you're batting in the Big League, and scoring every inning.

And when you're flippin' and ain't flappin, floppin' and ain't flyin' a-tall, you're short as my hair on knowing just what life really means. In fact, you're a first cousin to the Square, and a nephew of the Homey.

Low-quarters, my good man, are the footwear Lanes wear on the highways and byways of the land when they should wear hip boots. And when you collar a play that's righteous, really reecheous, or roacheous, as the case may be, you're as wild as a tenor sideman hunting a roach!

In slicing all corners, I know the short-cuts, and not playing you 14th Street means I'm not playing you cheap (you can get bargains down there, you know!). And the alternative to going to school is diggin' (reading) the information contained in newspapers (snitchpads).

Slicing your chops is a dignified way of beating your gums or doing a lot of talking. And the fine young hens tripping down the crunching straight, are just pretty gals out for a walk. And the larceny you're laying is the play you're making.

"You'd know all the fine points, if you were up on the stickers." And the hens out there are just muggin' (standing around) hoping that a Square like you will make a down payment on a fur jacket (dried barkers) or a dinner (scarf that won't choke 'em—presumably a heavier meal than cold cuts and crackers); or a glass with a little head on (a drink, my friend).

If I were in Siberia, I'd be on the shelf, and when I dig that you're shooting for the side-pocket and scratching every shot, I mean you're loud and wrong, although you mean well.

To "duck Uncle" is to avoid the draft (and I don't mean cold air).

"A righteous pad" is a place to sleep; "a scarf-ring trilly 'round the chimer" is to dine thrice daily.

"A mellow, young hen with feathers on her wings" is one who won't ask you for everything on the menu, and who'll do what she's told.

Do you dig?

OTHELLO, THE MOORE OF VENICE

As Conceived in Harlem Jive

ACT V, SCENE II

A Nod Box in the Rockpile (a bedroom in the castle)
Desdemona, the righteous wren, is stashed in her lilywhites.
    A light is burning.
Othello, the spade stud, pops in port, "down with it, 'cause he
    can't quit it."

Oth.—This is the action, this is the action, my tick-tock—
    I won't boot you to it, you unhipped flicks!
    This is the action.—Yet, I'll not gig
    This chick;
    Nor put down the wrong action on her
    Wheat rind,
    Grey as a ray in a blacken'd bottle.
    Yet this is the kiss-off for
    This banter, else she'll drop her
    Hype on other cats, mayhaps a Lane

43

From Spokane, or one who
Might be merely a Square, no doubt,
From Delaware, striving to locate
Madame St. Claire!
Stash the spark, and then, I say, Stash the spark!
If I put you down, thou mellow torch, I canst again lay the
    spark
On thee; Should I splash the salties: But once stash thy
    spark,
Thou mellow issue of truly in there slaving,
I know not where is that heavy heat,
That can spark thy torch again. When I have picked up on a rose,
I'm not with it to lay down the proper issue again; It must,
    ole man, get
Unglamorous:—I lay a sniff on this jive on the twig:—
[Here, Othello lays a hard-hitting mug act on the chick.]
    O mellow breath that almost makes me put it down like an
        unhipped Lane and stash away
My chib! One more, Fuzzy-Wuzzy, one more:—
Be thus, O babe, when thou hast been stashed
In thy deep six, and I will let thee hop a twig,
And splash my brine after thou has trilled:
One more, my mellow young hen, and this is the finale
I coppeth on this mushy, mugging jive:
So sweet was never so on the Jersey Side.
I must splash my salties:
But they are brinies, my queen, that are hipped to the play:
This weep act, ole man, is out of this world;
It tags me where it doth get groovy.
[Damn, Sam, the chick is snapping her peekers!]
Des.—Ah, 'tis my gallant Othello, ace of my spades;
    But, my good man, why doth thou dampen this
    Sleep suit of mine with thy brine?
    What are thou putting down; And, what is thy play?

Oth.—My queen, forsooth it is I; these salties that dothdampen
thy skin through yon booty
Gained from the clip act put down upon the sheep splash
now and anon for what I have stored
Deep in mine heart for thee; Truly, it is I, and I weep that I
shouldst bespoil thy
Slumber as must needs be, seeing that I have been booted
to sundry loose ends of hypes and
Jive, few cats who possess my perception canst latch on to.

Des.—Wilt thou stash thy fine brown frame on this righteous
softy with me, ole man, and let me soft gumbeat thee a bedtime fable?

Oth.—Wouldst rather that thou inclineth thine ear toward me
and diggeth these elements of jive that I wouldst put down
for thee to pick up;
Listen, Dessy, my fine young frail, Hast thou copped thy
plea to the Head Knock
Upstairs, this dim?

Des.—If thou beateth up thy gums about me putting down a
spiel to Him that Diggeth
Everything, I'm with it, pops!

Oth.—If thou canst lay a beg on thy conkpiece for any dash of
a flash of some unhipped hypes
Thou mighteth have put down, and thou has not,
As yet, laid down thy spiel to the Head Knock,
Chick, getteth thou with it!

Des.—Alas, Mister Man, what art thou gassing me with on an
issue such as that?

Oth.—Well, my queen, knock thyself a stoop on thy deuce of
prayer dukes, And, chick, maketh it
Short and snappy, that the twain of us canst be happy;
And while thou coppeth thy plea,
A bit of fine boogie-woogie shalt I get hipped to, meanwhile,
for I wouldst not knock thee off

When thou hast not latched onto thy beg; No,
Upstairs, pad of the Head Knock, forbid, I wouldst not
  knock off thy tick-tock!

Des.—Listen ole man; thou beateth out some weird off jive
  with thy blue gums; jive that
  Soundeth strange to these fine ears of mine; Let's git this
    mess straight:—
  Talketh thou of me copping my finale, or snipping out a
    paper dolly in the manner of one cutting out
  For good?

Oth.—O, my Queen, that seemeth to me most honorable, the
  thing, duty bound, I must, perforce, put down upon.

Des.—Then may the Head Knock put down a ladder from
  upstairs for me!

Oth.—Now, thou art with the issue, babe; thou art spieling
  with a feeling, and playeth not the dozens with thine
  Uncle's cousins.

Des.—If thou putteth down thy beef in that manner, ole man,
  I coppeth the issue that thou mighteth not gig me with thy
    chib; yon keen point thou has, in
  Days gone by, plucked ducks and jerk Turks!

Oth.—Still stash I here, O queen!

Des.—And yet, I am concerned, muchly so, that thou art up to
  some cutting and butting; For thou couldst not be in the
  mood for rooting and tooting
  As I wouldst have it in the manner we have put it down in
    past days of happy idyllism; for
  Thy brace of gims knock a spin: Why I shouldst feel so
    unglamorous, I canst not dig; Would that I
  Could lay a spiel to Madame St. Claire or others of those
    righteous old saws who knoweth much that
  Circles in conks such as thine; Truly, I canst not dig since I
    have not put down anything
  I couldst not again pick up; Jeeze, Jake, I feel like the snake,
    and too, so unnecessary!

46

Oth.—Knock thy wig, chick, for the hypes thou has put
down.

Des.—Listen ole man; all yon Jive I have spread only has been
put down to knock thee a Benny when

Mister Hawkins rides his December chariot; or when he
plucketh the eider feathers of the sky

Geese and scattereth them upon this twirling Apple and
maketh thou to twitch and twitch and gas

Lightly, yet so politely,—brrrr, 'tis cold as Hell; forsooth,
my jive has commercial aspects,

In that 'tis put down to knock thee a scoff when thine own
scoffings art slim; and we twain, perforce, must

Cop our goo from such unglamorous fare as fish-heads,
wherein we also scramble for the gills,

Or scoff on onions, our gims, meanwhile, being wiped with
our bunch of fives with much anguish and

Painful gusto! Why talketh thou of my hypes? 'Tis all in
thy favor.

Oth.—So I diggeth, O babe; 'Tis also the reason that I giggeth
thee.

Des.—That Salt River action, ole man, is so unglamorous, so
Unhipped; Especially when 'tis put down on a mush and
mug play; Damn, Jackson, thou art knocking a

Scoff on thy chops! Something booteth me that thou art
not switching an' twitching for naught; I'm hipped

That thou art putting down the action that mighteth latch
onto me as the main play.

Oth.—Don't beat up thy chops, so much, chick!

Des.—All right, Poppa-Stoppa; all-reet, all-root, all-rut!

Oth.—That blower I dropped on thee which on me was
dropped by my papa's old saw; the same that my illustrious
sire copped such a slave to

Dig the Dead Presidents required for its acquisition; Thou,
O lowlife broad,

Laid upon that cat, Cassio.

Des.—Well, I'll be damned! That, old man, is the wrong play;
Send for the stud and put the bee on him.

Oth.—Listen here, chick: I'm hipped and booted to all plays:
Diggeth thou how these boots do rise beyond my deuce of
benders? Thou shouldeth know that I am an old boot
wearer; thou art, my fine young hen, about ready for that
cold meat party.

Des.—I diggeth what thou putteth down; but not this finale
copping jive.

Oth.—Thou art not one who couldst revel in the uncertain
glories of being, what in the vile vernacular is call'd a hipped
chick:
Thou art due for thy back slammer cutout: Therefore, my
Queen,
Thou mayest lay the real jive down for me about this foul
hype thou didst try to lay on the hyper;
For to beat up thy gums and make me dig thee like a square,
cannot put the jive down on me
That thou are a Perfect Lamb. Babe, thou
Art to knock thy broom to the Jersey Side, where,
With Old Man Mose, thou wilt sciffle and scuffle,
But won't get back.

Des.—Then may the Head Knock layeth gims on me.

Oth.—Backeth I that spiel, Babe; I, Othello, the Spade
Stud, is on the beam on that play.

Des.—Well, old man, since thou art to send me a love letter;
and thou art so close
By me, thou art the one whose gims
Shouldeth beam with a more kindly light
On me: Listen, Mister Man, never did I put
Down action that thou couldst not fall out in mellow
Bull's wool, nor
Knock thy goo on a zoom, wherewithal in
Such issues there must needs be a

Slave action put down; I couldst never come up
On a stud like that Lane, Cassio. And old
Man, I never laid any of thy mellow goods
Upon him.

Oth.—Don't try to jive me, chick; didst not I dig the stud toot-
ing his sneezer into the blower
I knocked thee to? O, thou lying hen,
Thou dost put the bang act on my ticker, and mak'st me to
    put down this action as a
Boom-boom play, when I wouldst have gigged thee with
My Harlem toothpick. Babe, I dug the stud with my snorter.

Des.—Well, the cat must have picked up on it; I couldst not
have been so unbooted as to let you see
Him with it when it was so hard for you to get it; Spiel,
Othy, for the stud to trilly here; let him put down the real
    riff on this issue.

Oth.—The stud hast booted me to the play, Babe; he spieled
that the jive was dropped on him by thee.

Des.—What jiveth thou now, Mister Man?

Oth.—That he hath dropped his hype on thee.

Des.—How? In what manner? Doth thou mean I laid it upon
him on a zoom; a tab act in the unhipped manner of a chick
on her first tour of the turf?

Oth.—That is what thou diddeth, O babe.

Des.—Cassio wouldst not put down that spiel where I couldst
dig it; 'twould be unrighteous for such to come to pass.

Oth.—Nope. He canst not spiel enty more; That Square,
Iago, put the oil act on him once I hipped him to the issue.

Des.—That sounds as groovy, Old Man, as a ten cent movie; is
the stud, Cassio, up Salt River?

Oth.—O, my queen, that square, Iago, is down with the action,
built on a solid half-traction; they don't come back, once his
brace of hookers have been put upon them!

Des.—Now isn't this a damned shame; the stud wast not to blame,

And here I'm trying to beg a lift out of this unrighteous riff;
Sorry, Mister Man, but I must put down a brine play;
Weep I must for that fine grey.

Oth.—Now ain't this some mad mess? Honest, I diggeth not thee,
Des. The chick is putting down with the salt over that stud,
Cassio,
Right to my pan; What's this unhipped jive thou trieth
thine hardeth to lay on me, chick?
Truly, I dig thee not.

Des.—Old man, thou canst put the slammer acton me and
I, thereupon, wilt cop my trot; But, please, don't put the
hush-hush act on me;
I'm really ready, My fine Mister Freddie, but I wouldst rather
Knock a drill, not lay up here, all quiet and still.

Oth.—Down, thou low, unglamorous wren.

Des.—I'll tell thee like the farmer informed the 'tater: Planteth
me now, diggeth I thee later;
Listen, pops, you mayst call the cops; Pipe down on the
rooting and tooting; There existeth no real need for
booting and shooting; I'll dig my drapes and righteous
capes, and collar my drill
With a hurry-up trill; I'll even snip a dolly,
Just like my Aunt Polly, in this mad, frantic dim,
And, old man, I'll drop my hype on both ends of the stem;
But, Mister Man, please don't gig me now; Hey Lawdy,
Poppa,
Please don't Gig me now!

Oth.—Naw, Babe: Too much gold have I laid upon thee; Each
Dead President have I taken that thou has put in my deuce
Of grabbers; And put the fruits of such filthy, tho'
Welcome green upon thy righteous frame; O, I knoweth that
I am a solid cat; a stud groomed in all the answers, may-
haps, the questions, too; And hipped am I that this stud,
Cassio was a mellow lad, who put it down with all he had;

But, thou, my fine, pink banter, Art
Thou not brought down by thine own unbooted
Action in which thou figureth not out each play
And leaveth loose ends, such as the blower thou
Beat that John for on the ace dim of the backbeat
Thirty? If thou hadst cut out from the
Roach as I thought thou hadst,
My chib would not be so fain to gig thee
As 'tis right now.

Des.—Mister Man, Mister Man: let me drop to my double
bumpers and cop a plea to the Head
Knock that
I mighteth find a squat Upstairs when I
Push my broom up the
Blue Broadway.

Oth.—Thou hadst thy chance, chick. I wilt not mess up this
mellow blue chib, hammer'd out from finest of Damascus
blue steel; Instead, my double fives about thy stretcher,
Place I thus: and with a light crush act,
Trilly, babe, that is thy
Play.

Here I Come with my Hair Blowing Back

In "laying spiels," one is sometimes tempted, like a mountain climber, to attempt to scale the verbal heights, and although such an effort may prove disastrous and the goal unattained, the attempt is infinitely worth-while. As an example of a kind of Jive contrapuntal, a means of practicing the fine and intricate art of Jive talk, I have included this one:

In reality this title might seem a gross misrepresentation of fact since my locks are quite short, and show no indication of blowing either backward or forward. However, the use of this expression in Jive is "strictly in the groove," and as a further follow-up, I would point out to you that, "When the wind blows the other way, Cholly Hoss, my moss gets in my eyes. I'm in a solid groove, ole man, as groovy as a grade A movie; and I'm liable to 'blow my top' doing the Back Bay Hop. Now, I know you're righteous, because the cat I dug laying his spiel in the house of many slammers told me you'd be. On that account I'm gonna slay you with some fine hep-jive. I'm gonna slap some chops, and come up with one of those plays you latch on to when you're roaming in the gloaming."

Jive, in order to be practiced properly, must have the proper background, the proper atmosphere, like any other art. For instance, we're in a somber, blue-lighted room. The rug is thick and there are couches with soft pillows against the walls. There's a mellow, righteous record being played on the piccolo; and, if you listen closely, you'll dig that it's the Hawk, knocking out that heavy and frantic melody of "Body and Soul" on that tenor saxophone of his. Every cat and chippie is "teed" up high, and calling for chocolate and peppermint candy. The Lady Who Runs the House is passing around little glasses filled with bright red wine, so, ole man, who cares about anything outside? Who cares?

Says one cat, his shoes lying at his side—

"Ole man, it's mellow if you get frantic, and it's fine if you're wild. Jackson, a roach ain't nothing but a roach; and when it's brown the light gets bluer, and the music sends you right out of this world. And you don't have to belong to the U.S.A.A.F. to go 'way up high. I'm in the groove, and I'm gonna lay a little spiel on you about a chippie I once knew. This chippie, Stud Hoss, was a bringdown, but Jackson, I'm tangled like the rope, lost in love but without hope. Her hair, ole man, was short and nappy, but Cholly Hoss, she sure was happy. Nope. Not much to gim, sorta beat as to her limbs, but I'm fluttering every time I dig her. See this roach? Ole man, I didn't pick it up under the kitchen sink. The chippie started me. She was a viper, the only one like her; and she got high from there to nigh.

"I was a Solid Square. My boots were always opened, and slipped off when I walked. She showed me how to lace them up properly; how to wear them to my hips. She was righteous, ole man, truly righteous. In fact, all root, to the final toot. I, as a Homeboy, always had my umbrella, like a simple fella. I'd hang my head, bow it in shame, if a pretty chick called me by name.

"If a cat laid a spiel on me, I'd run home for my dictionary. I couldn't collar what they were laying down when they'd ask me to 'cop a squat' or 'slice my chops.' And I couldn't dig when they'd want me to 'knock a scoff,' or 'weed 'em a brace of chollies.' I thought a 'skybird' was a dove. A carpet, ole man, understand, I thought was a plain rug. I thought 'lush' was water with the 's' left off. But this chippie really hipped me, booted me to the play. Here's part of her daily spiel to me:

"'You ain't a Square. You're really somewhere. You're in your boots to your 'twice-five' roots. Your line is fine; in fact, divine; but, boy, don't wade out too deep, 'cause the sharks play 'em for keeps! Don't be no pearl diver, when you can be a mighty fine jiver! If you can't fly, don't get high. When you sing, always chirp the verse; otherwise, you might need a nurse; since the chorus is mighty tough for cats who can't dig the stuff. And, Jackson, when you smoke, drink a little coke—and always remember that your play is broke.'

"Now, ole man, thanks to her, I'm hipped. When I hear you say, 'Let's trilly long down the cruncher!' I know that you mean 'let's take a walk.' When you mention a 'deuce o' demons,' I know you mean a couple of dimes. When you say 'dive for pearls,' I know you mean a job washing dishes. When you mention 'Squares in Their Chairs,' you mean Congressmen. And when you say 'trotters,' you mean 'pig's feet.'

"If I hear you beefing about ruffles, I know you aren't spieling about some girl's dress, but about good old chitterlings. An ace-deuce means three; and a tray and a solo means four; and a five-spot is an eggplant; and when you double an eggplant, it's breadfruit. A goola is a piano. A lamb is a lane, and a lane is a square, and a square is a homey, and a homey ain't nowhere—just like the bear's brother. Jim, for him the pickin's are slim.

"Now when a cat talks about his chippie, he means his chick; and chick means broad, and a broad means hen; and hen means saw; and saw means 'Fuzzy-Wuzzy,' a solid, little huzzy. Cats get their moss to lay down flat by taking the top of their chippie's legsack, and putting a knot, and a demon in it, then sleeping in it all night with a solid pound of some fine lay-me-down, then come up in the early bright with a conk that's truly all right. When you talk about flat sponges, you mean avenue tripe. But Norwegian lard really isn't at all hard. You see, Jackson, this roach has got me rising. In fact, I'm flying. Dig you when I come down."

You may get a bit involved on this one, but from now on, you're on your own. We might go into detailed discussions of the various phrases, words and terms, but the play now is for you to "pick up" and "dig" this mess all by your own, pretty self, but are you pretty, or only a hepcat from Kansas City?

I might clarify things a little, however, by mentioning the fact that 'The Hawk' is Coleman Hawkins, famous saxophonist; that a roach is a reefer, and a reefer is a weed, and a weed is gage, and gage is a torch, and a torch is charge, and charge is marijuana. A "skybird" is a hallucination of the mind, in which one visualizes such creatures, and notes to one's horror that the "skybird" is minus feathers and a motor. "Chitterlings" are the entrails of a hog, cleansed thoroughly, boiled, or fried, and served with cornbread, plus a bottle of beer.

Everyone knows that life isn't half as thrilling, as exciting, or as picturesque as it should be. Jive undertakes to remedy that situation with language that makes up for the dullness of mere existence. The following is a

Portrait of a Hepcat Getting "Sharp"

Ole man, I'm down with it, found with it, bound with it, around with it, and gowned with it. In other words, I'm a hip kitty from New Yawk City; ain't it a pity you ain't quite as witty? Ole man, never be as dull as the average skull! Brighten your corner, Poppa Do Wrong, and chirp your song, 'cause it won't be long 'fore Uncle sounds the gong!

Ole man, you've gotta get sharp. You cop a light splash, not too heavy, Stud Hoss, if it's the four and one (you dig the dip, Jackson, on the four and two!). Then you lay down some action with the smoke-screen under your brace of hookers. Dig yourself a groundpad bag; tie up a sou in the big end and when you've mowed your lawn righteously with that Jesse James Killer; lay your mellow roof into the sack and twist the sou into a knot which you next turn up under the edge of the bag. Then, ole man, lay plenty of that ofay-sweet smell all over your fine brown frame; and then, and only then, do you lay your broom to the slammer that fronts the drape crib and split it slightly and politely, and let your gims dig until you get the beam. When you put down this action, quite ready (No Joke says Moke and Poke!), your deuce of peekers will lamp the sock-frock, and all you need do then is to stash your trotters into those bluff cuffs with the solid sender parachute benders. If it is the cute suit, with the loop droop, you're playing the game, really ole man, quite the same, and the chicks will surely dig your name. Then you knock yourself a white one with the high hard yard. To be really groovy, Stud Hoss, you put down on the streamer issue and pick up on a good latch for the gate to your front yard and then you ease into your racket-jacket with the mellow drag, that has the sag. You next lay one of those long ones with many links onto your squeezer and hook it into your rathole. Slip on a pair of howling knitwear. Then you latch onto a groundpad spade and ease your brace of horned corns into your dagger pointed goldies. Then, ole man, you pick up a flyer with the roof slightly higher, and, pops, when you look into your gazer you'll be sharp just like a razor, and really glad you look so mad.

JIVE PSALM OF LIFE

(Apologies to Henry Wadsworth Longfellow)

Jive me not in unhipped numbers
Life is but a righteous nod—
And that cat is stiff and dumber
Planting water in the sod.

———

Jive is real! Jive is mellow!
And the six is not its end—
Dig a chick that's fine and yellow
Then thy gold thou must then spend!

———

Not some balling, not a bringdown,
Is the cut out on this play—
But to hype all fools around me
Finds me turfing for my hay.

———

Hustling's hard, the tick is tocking—
And our clocks, all in the groove—
Dig the skinbeat, it is rocking,
Jack, it's up to you to move!

———

In the apple's turf of scuffling
In the bivouac of hemp—
Be not unhipped in the shuffling
Cut your rug if ye must limp!

———

Nix the offbeat, Jack, play the game
Let the backbeat cop a trot—
Put it down now for gold and fame—
Tick-tock inward, here I'll squat.

———

Lives of great cats oft do jive us
We can hustle like they did—
And in trilling, stash behind us
Groundpads on the righteous mid.

THE BOOK OF HYPES

The use of nicknames in Jive and American slang is recognized by linguistic authorities as an indication of the mood of light-hearted joviality and carefree abandon, habitual with those who use it. These nicknames in Jive eloquently portray the Negro's aptitude for creating word pictures as pointed out in the foregoing quotation from Miss Hurston's work.[6] Would there be a more telling character portrayal than that found in such names as "Dime Begging Shorty"? or "Fuzzy Wuzzy, a Wild Little Huzzy"?

As a study in personality of two such picturesque individuals, we shall herewith deal with the following "groovy" dialogue between Joe Q. Hipp, the Stroll's Last Dip, and Sam D. Home, Just Here From Rome.

Joe Hipp, as his name implies, is an expert in talking Jive, the understanding of which gives him character and standing among his associates.

Same D. Home is not a Square; instead, he's one of the boys on the corner, fastidious regarding his attire, vain of his appearance, mentally alert and quite capable of taking care of himself in any fistic or verbal encounter.

Joe Q. Hipp, the Stroll's Last Dip, and Sam D. Home, Just Here From Rome, were standing on a corner in Harlem one day. Overhead the warm spring sunshine flooded them with its benign and effulgent rays, inspiring them to speech and impelling them to share mutual confidences. Joe Hipp wore a wide-brimmed hat which shadowed his built-up athletic shoulders, a hat encompassed with a broad, zebralike band of black and white. His suit was a simple, single-breasted affair, "solid" sky blue in color, as gaudy as a circus-wagon. The wide shoulder accented Joe's narrow waist line; and the jacket struck a curve over his hips which ended five inches from his knees. His trousers were a mere forty inches at the knee and a fanatical fourteen inches at the ankle! His shoes were a bright yellow in color with the toes upturned at an impish angle.

Sam D. Home's attire leaned a bit more to the conservative side, befitting the respectability implied by his name. The brim of his hat was a good inch or two narrower than that of his more radical friend, Joe Hipp. His suit was made of brown pin-striped material. His shoulders, like those of his companion, were also built up to the exaggerated style affected by the zoot-suiters, and his waistline was also narrow. His jacket did not descend quite as low as Joe's. His trousers were thirty inches at the knee, and twenty at the ankle. His shoes were grey suedes, but minus the freakish toes which characterized the shoes worn by his dapper and more flashily attired friend.

Their conversation, once safely past the initial stages, turned naturally enough to the subject of women. The following dialogue ensued—

Joe Q. Hipp—Whatcha know, ole man, whatcha know?

Sam D. Home—Man, I know from nothin'. What you know?

Joe Q. Hipp—I dunno, ole man, understand? I'm trying to find out something. Whatcha know?

Sam D. Home—I been taking it on the downbeat, soft and low, taking my time and playing it slow. How the chicks treating you?

Joe Q. Hipp—You know, ole man, I cops all plays and digs all lays, understand, ole man? I'm still Joe Hipp, the Stroll's Last Dip, and I won't slip if I leave my ship. Tune in your mikes and dig this right. I'm stiffing on the stroll on the late dark a deuce or tray of haircuts on the backbeat, when I latched on to this hard, mad spiel about the chippie and the cat that cracks the whip.

"The way the jive was dropped on me, a deuce o' squares were knocking themselves out in the lush-pad on the three pointer and slicing their chops real awful about the way that skull, Hitler, and his Johns are kicking the gong around in the layout across the drink, when in drills a chippie with grass as short as mine. Ole man, understand, one of them homies dug her, understand, as she popped into port.

"He lamped her straight up and down, understand, Home, and then mugged behind five to his Jasper-boy. She's sorta mellow, ole man, understand, and I'm gonna lay some deep-sugar on her and see if it will melt. Dig them pins and latch on to that hide. Them glimmers stand out like meat balls in onion gravy. She's a gasser, Jack, understand?[7]

"The other cat's playing the bear's brother, Freddie, but all the time he's ready, understand? Well, the chippie stashes her frame on a pig-hide and digs the dipper for some brine, laying a thin on the line. She's got the cutware bottoms up, and it's gurgling, ole man, understand, when the first Square makes his play. He spiels—

"'Listen, Babes, you're really in there, understand? You're

laying your knowledge and picking up the fruit. You're righteous and you ought to shout for joy, understand? But, Babes, you ain't nowhere without your proper Square. You're playing the dozens with your uncle's cousins, but you're like the marsh-mellow, all soft 'n' yellow. I'm the jive you gotta dig. I can make your pad soft as butter, cause I'm a solid carpet cutter, but you gotta come to school, understand? I'll see that you knock a scoff, ace-deuce around the ticker, but you gotta let me be the slicker, understand? I'll crack all whips, you cop all trips!'

And here's what the chippie said to the square—

"'Listen, homey, you don't know me, but I'm making my plays on the run. I'm Diamond Lily, and you're just plain Willie. I want my jelly on a bun. You're in here gassing, while the black is passing, and the world goes round and round. I'll admit I'm a chippie, here from Mississippi, but you're wrong when you play me cheap. I dig all plays from roundabout ways, and my jive goes down real deep. I'm laying my racket, can't you dig this packet? Why should I dance on a dime? You're loud and whipped, you're sure to get clipped; your clock is keeping the wrong time'."

Sam D. Home—'Twas a righteous spiel, ole man, and I dug it straight up and down, three ways sides and flats, straight across the board.

TO HELP YOU GET A COMPLETE PICTURE OF THIS, HERE IS WHAT WAS MEANT BY WHAT WAS SAID—

Joe Q. Hipp—"Well, what did I say?"

Sam D. Home—"When you said you 'copped all plays and dug all lays,' you meant you had your eyes and ears peeled for every bit of the conversation and action you were relating.

When you told me to 'tune in my mikes,' you meant that I should listen attentively to what you had to say. What you said was simply that you were standing on the corner one night two or three weeks ago when you heard the story you just told me, about the pretty glamour girl and the playboy who doesn't work if he can help it. At the time the story opens, two fellows were having some drinks in the corner bar and talking about that heel, Hitler, and his side kicks in Europe stirring up so much trouble, when the glamour girl with her hair clipped short, and slicked down on her skull entered. One of the two fellows saw her as she came in and looked her over slowly and then whispered behind his hand to his companion: 'She's very nice looking and I'm going to try and make a bid for her attention, and see if she can be approached. Look at her legs and the texture of her skin. Her eyes are large and bright. She's perfect, my friend'."

"You said," Sam D. Home continues, shifting the weight of his body to the other leg, "that the other fellow tried to appear disinterested, but in reality he was all eyes and ears. The girl seated herself on a stool and asked the bartender for a glass of beer which cost her a dime. She was drinking this when the first young man spoke his piece. He said: 'Listen, baby, you're really something to look at. You evidently are using your very seductive charms to advantage, and because of that you are indeed a singular individual. But you are missing a lot in life without the right type of boy friend. You're doing everything wrong, despite the fact that while you're young and pretty, you aren't getting the ultimate satisfaction from life you would if you knew me better. I can make things pleasant for you because I know everything, have been everywhere, and can get you the things you want, but you must listen to me. I'll see that you eat three good meals a day, but you must let me be the big boss. In other words, I'll instruct, you obey.'

"The girl said— 'Listen, my simple friend, you don't know me. But I know just what I'm doing. I'm really a smart woman while you're rather dumb. The man I take up my time with must be more representative. You're in here running your mouth while the night is passing and the world goes round and round. I'll admit I'm a glamour girl and look as though I just came to town, but you're wrong when you play me cheap. I understand everything that's going on, and you'd be surprised at the things I've forgotten that you don't know. I'm living my life, can't you see my well-filled purse? Why should I jump at your command? You're very uncouth and certainly you don't know much, consequently, you're in danger of being taken advantage of.'

"Well, Joe Hipp, did I dig you that time, ole man?"

Joe Q. Hipp—"Ole man, you were in there, I mean, in there."

In using the above expressions found in the dialogue between Joe Q. Hipp and Sam D. Home, the reader should refer to the following lexicon—

"Cop a squat" means "to sit."

"Tune in your mikes" means "to listen."

"Heavy lard" refers to a story to be told.

"Stiffing on the stroll" means "standing on the street."

"Late black" refers to late night.

"A deuce of haircuts on the back beat" means two or three weeks before.

"Chippie" means glamour girl, play girl.

"Cat that cracks the whip" means playboy, sportman.

"A deuce of squares" means two rather average fellows with an overbalanced belief in their ability to move about in fast company.

"Lush pad on the three pointer" refers to the saloon on the corner.

"Slicing their chops" means talking.

"Layout across the drink" refers to the continent of Europe.

"Grass" designates short hair.

"Mugged behind five" means talking behind the palm of his hand.

"Deep sugar" means sweet talk.

"Pins" are legs.

"Hides," smooth skin.

"Glimmers," eyes.

"Gasser," really tops.

"Stashes her frame on a pig-hide," sits on a leather-covered stool.

"Digs the dipper from some brine" means she asked the bartender for a beer.

"Cutware bottoms up" means glass turned up in the process of drinking.

"Thin on the line" means paying a dime across the counter.

"Laying your knowledge" means taking advantage of a situation.

"Playing the dozens with one's uncle's cousins" means doing everything wrong.

"Scoff, ace-deuce around the ticker" means three square meals daily.

I hope, dear reader, that you are paying strict attention to the matter of your diction as you advance in the complicated undertaking of correctly assimilating and using Organic Jive.

The functional difficulties that you may have encountered in attempting to apply the knowledge you have attained in Organic Jive should disappear as you acquire a wider command of this new and fascinating adjunct to the English tongue.

The dialogue between Joe Q. Hipp and Sam D. Home was written to give you a further illustration as to the use of Jive as a means of amusing conversation. In the next scene we encounter Joe Q. Hipp kicking the conversational gong around in company with his seductive girl friend "Fuzzy-Wuzzy a Wild Little Huzzy." I would suggest that you analyze this carefully, studying it for style and content, then check your impression of what is actually being said with the definitions in the lexicon in the back of this book,[8] remembering what you have already learned (or did you merely glance at it?) regarding Jive Verbs, Jive Nouns and Adjectives, Jive Rhymes, Phrases both Simile and Hyperbole.

Joe Q. Hipp—"Listen, Babes, I ain't got no fame, but I'm playin' the game. I'm a Square; got a dime to spare? I wanna snicker, got any likker? I'm from the righteous halfworld that lives on jump. Dig me?"

Fuzzy-Wuzzy—"Jack, you're trying to lay a hype as if you wanted tripe. Don't lay no unhipped spiels on me. You're more frantic than pedantic. Spiel to me and spiel hard. I'm in the proper frame to listen to how you play your game. Spiel, pops, spiel!"

Joe Q. Hipp—"I dug a chippie on the early G and she booted me to a righteous play. So, on the early beam, I trumped the hump, and, ole man, I was in the mood to jump since I'd been blowin' the joy roots all the solid dim. I stiffs the stroll for a deuce of ticks and then latches onto a gatemouth with his hair blowing back. Ole gatemouth is romping. In fact, he was feeling his weight and he digs me and I digs him and then he spiels—

"'Look out. Cholly-Hoss; are you all rote, like the letter, or all-rate like the taxicab?'

"I spiels back and lays him with this—

"'Man, I'm as chipper as the China Clipper and in the mood to play. You're out here gassing while the black is passing. I'm trying to blow my troubles away.'

Spiels the gatemouth—

"'You'll just be in time at a quarter 'round nine, and if you're right, you're bright. I just came out from the House Without Chairs Where the Lights are a Solid Blue. If you're hipped, you won't get clipped; but if you're a Lane, you'll be caught in the rain, 'cause the chippies there play it hard. I thought you were a solid hipcat, but here I find you're just the same as a simple name, missing your time at bat. It's on the third floor and at the rear is the door. You ring the bell twice to get your swimps and wice.'

"That's where I cut out, Babes, 'cause I'm on the beat to play. I digs the pile of bricks and collars a duster up the ladder and lays it hard on the tinkle. I waits for about six ticks and then I latch on that somebody is gimming me from a peeper in the slammer. I lets 'em dig me all over, Babes. I twisted 'round like I was the revolving man and lets them latch on to that hard drape I'm in, and let 'em dig them stomps and that sky and that pair of pistols I'm sporting at my ankles.

"They must've seen I'm fine as vines producing green wines 'cause they flip the twister an' open the slammer and I pops in port. I can't dig this mess. The midway in the layout is as blue as 'My Mamma Done Tole Me,' and I'm trying to gun them open slammers on the midway where I hear the Hawk riding and latch on to the chippies giggling.

"I digs the saw that knocked me in, and babes, I can't cop her map, although it looks sorta grey to me, although I did dig them hams, that takeoff and them gams.

"Fuzz, she collars a duster down the midway and cops a stop in front of one of them pads with the slammer half split. It's like cheese, but I ain't got my chib so I eases in and cops a squat on the soft-top near the wall. Next to me is a fine young bantam and she's getting all sticky and tricky with some peppermint candy.

"Fuzz, that grass was like a forest fire, and all I can dig is a lot of coughing and puffing and blowing and see a lot of lightning bugs moving round in the solid blue. Then when my peeks dig the range, I'm booted that I'm in the ballroom without a parachute.

"And, Fuzz, none of these fine young fryers all squatting on them fine soft-tops is got a parachute, so I knocks it out in my knowledge box that the best thing for me to do is to lay a trey of sous and a double ruff on the head hen and knock some joy for myself. Well, the head chick pulls a Rudolf Hess, and hikes for some mess, and in about three ticks is back with it. I snaps a snapper with my short finger and then I'm puffing and coughing and blowing and getting mellow as a Viennese cello with the rest. All the time, my fine young bantam, I don't dig no colts and can't cop the play with a crib full of fillies and the table set and no scoff. So I starts in laying a soft spiel on the bantam with the peppermint candy. She wants me to knock a piece, but I'm booted to my armpits and digs the play that if she gives me now, she's solid gonna lay a beg later, and you know about the farmer and the 'tater.

"Well, just when I'm getting groovy as a Bogart movie, I digs a heavy play on the tinkle that ain't the way they toot up for scofftime. The head chick starts up the midway, and then does a Rommel right back again, and pops in the pad and chirps that we'd better put out the fire, cause the man who rides the screaming gasser is in port. Well, babes, there was all kinds of jumping and thumping and romping and stomping going on, and it's then that I dig that all that's in the House Without Chairs Where the Lights Are a Solid Blue are a bunch of Gal Officers, Harpies, Stewers and Chicks That Play It Hard. I was half a stretch away when they started marching."

Fuzzy-Wuzzy replies—"That's more like Joe Q. Hipp, foxy as a freebie to the Roxy. Solid, ole man."

The translation of this for the absolutely lazy is as follows—

Joe Q. Hipp wants to tell Fuzzy-Wuzzy about a unique experience which befell him recently. But, rather impatiently,

she informs him that he is merely taking up her time with a lot
of pointless talking. Joe continues. He says he met a girl early
in the evening who told him about a place where things were
exciting, and the company would be to his liking. The words
in his soliloquy to watch are—

Booted me—introduced me to, or informed me of
Early beam—early hour
Trumped the hump—climbed the hill
Joy roots—reefers, marijuana cigarettes
Gatemouth—one who knows everyone else's business
House Without Chairs Where the Lights are a Solid Blue—a
　　goodtime flat, ballroom, shady rendezvous
Clipped—have one's bankroll taken
Swimps and wice, shrimps and rice—a way of saying that
　　one can get what he wants
Collars a duster up the ladder—climb the steps
Tinkle—doorbell
Gimming—looking one over
Slammer—door
Drape—zoot suit
Stomps—shoes
Sky—hat
Pistols—zoot trousers
Twister—key
Pops in port—enter
Midway—hallway
Layout—house
The Hawk riding—refers to Coleman Hawkins, famous
　　saxophonist, playing his popular "Body and Soul" on a
　　phonograph record

Gun—look over
Saw—landlady
Map—face
Hams—thighs
Takeoff—hips
Gams—legs
Like cheese—odor
Chib—knife
Soft-top—stool
Grass-reefers—marijuana
Lightning-bugs—lighted cigarettes in a darkened room
Peeks dig the range—eyes take in the scene
Ballroom without a parachute—in a reefer den without
  reefers
Fine fryers—pretty young girls, chicks
Knowledge-box—brain
Trey of sous and a double ruff—forty cents
Head hen—landlady
Rudolph Hess—fade away
Snap a snapper—light a match
Young bantam—little girl
Colts—young boys
Crib full of fillies—room full of young girls and women
Groovy—settling into a comfortable stance, mood
Rommel—did an about face, like the Nazi general
Fire—cigarettes
Man who rides the screaming gasser—police patrol
Gal officers, harpies—lesbians
Stewers—old women
Chick that plays it hard—glamour girl
Half a stretch away—half a block

You may have noted in the above spiel involving Joe Q. Hipp and his girl friend, Fuzzy-Wuzzy, that they made use of the jive verb, "booted." To be "hipped" is one thing all jivers strive to be, but to be "booted" is the essence of the entire frame-work of the system of organic jive. It is to be "out of this world," indeed. It is something like having rehearsed a selection in elocution in the privacy of one's own room, then gathering courage, to have performed it for a small audience in the parlor, and meeting with success, finally getting a chance to perform in an amphitheatre before thousands of people.

The fellow who is "hipped" or "hepped" is common, indeed. But one who is "booted" is an unique individual, indeed.

The background of this all-purpose verb "boot" has its roots deep in the structural foundations of the entire system. To be hipped, one has to have his boots on. The tighter the boots are laced, the more hipped the wearer is supposed to be. Now, I hope you are not confusing the boots of which I speak, and which all jivers know about and worship with whole-hearted devotion, with the more common variety of cowhide, or leather of any description. If you are, then, Brother, you are mistaken indeed.

Like the Red Slippers which the Good Fairy presented to Dorothy in "The Wizard of Oz," you don't see the jiver's boots at all, unless you are blessed with phenomenal imagination. In fact, there are none to see. The really "booted cat" might be bare-foot and yet have on a pair of furlined boots of priceless texture and workmanship. For, you see, "boots" in the Jive sense are mental. Purely mental. "I'm booted, ole man" refers to a state of mind, and at the same time, confuses the "unbooted" person who might accidentally overhear the conversation. Thus your true and artistic Jiver takes pleasure in bewildering the rest of mankind as he "grooves" himself and "lays his spiel."

In "grooving" oneself, there is a definite physical action involved; a lazy, quick motion of both shoulders describing a kind of short, over-handed arc, as though one were shrugging the shoulders like a prize-fighter skipping rope. At the same time, the body takes on a languid kind of stance, with the knees bent slightly, or deeply, depending on the amount of "grooving" the "groover" is inclined to exhibit. His hands are busy pulling the lapels of the coat together, or, in varied instances, pointing groundward with a quivering forefinger sticking out like a divining rod. This action is usually performed on the street corner, in front of the theatre, in the candy store, or in corners of the ballroom in full view of those whose boots are not on, and who wouldn't know how to lace them up properly if they were on.

In laying his spiel, the Jiver, who has by now sufficiently "grooved" himself, gives forth in conversation some of the highlights of the language we have already discussed, which lifts him out of the ranks of the plain "hipped" into the halls of those who wear their boots laced up tight.

"Boot" is another verb of commendation and approval. I "boot" you to a stranger, means I introduce you to someone. "I'm booted to what you're saying," means I understand the trend of your conversation. No one ever put over anything on a person who was "booted" to all plays and lays. It is simply impossible these days to take advantage of a cat who is booted, because said cat is ready to meet all situations, cases, and emergencies. His spiels are all correct and in the accepted standards of Jive. His clothes are the latest thing in the modern mood, whether "zooted" or "tooted."

The ultimatum, however, is to wear "fur-lined boots." This is the peak of Jive perfection. That there are very few in this class is easy to understand since very few of the booted cats and chicks have sufficient imagination, sense of words and rhyming, to rise to this state of glory.

JIVE JOYCE KILMER'S "TREES"

I think that I shall never dig
A spiel as righteous as a twig.
A twig whose scoffish chops are stashed
Right on the apple's pile of trash.
A twig that digs the knock each bright
And spreads its hooks so fine and right.
A twig, Jack, that may in heat time drape
A crib of feathers in its cape.
Upon whose barrel Hawk has squat
Who is so mellow on each spot.
Spiels are laid by lanes like me
But just the Knock can make a tree.

The Technique of Jive

LESSON NO. 1

"If you're a hipped stud, you'll latch on; but if you're a homey, you ain't nowhere, ole man, understand? Like the bear, nowhere. And, ole man, why can't you dig this hard mess I'm laying down when the whole town's copping the mellow jive? Are you going to be a square all your days? Ain't you gonna click your gimmers, latch onto this fine pulp I'm dropping on you and really knock yourself out as you scoff, ace-deuce around the chiming Ben? You dig, ole man, that, from early bright to late black, the cats and the chippies are laying down some fine, heavy jive; most of it like the tree, all root; like the letter all wrote; like the country road, all rut; like the apple, all rot; like the cheese, all rat! Understand, ole man?"

That, dear reader, is pure jive. However, we'll play around with it and translate that paragraph later. Don't worry, we'll come back to it.

1. Introduction to Basic Jive

Before entering on the details of the System of Basic Jive, it seems appropriate to answer here those general questions and inquiries which everyone hearing of Jive for the first time is inclined to ask. These questions may be summed up roughly as follows:

How and why the System developed? How the principles on which it is evolved have been established? What are the needs and purposes which it professes to serve, the methods by which it may be learned, its value to the individual, its place in education, the agencies through which it may be spread, and its advantages as an auxiliary medium of expression?

I. What Is Jive?

Jive is a distortion of that staid, old, respectable English word "jibe" (jibber—Speak fast and inarticulately, shatter; such speech or sound. Jibberish—unintelligible speech, meaningless sounds, jargon, blundering or ungrammatical talk).

In the sense in which it came into use among Negroes in Chicago about the year 1921, it meant to taunt, to scoff, to sneer—an expression of sarcastic comment. Like the tribal groups of Mohammedans and people of the Orient, Negroes of that period had developed a highly effective manner of talking about each other's ancestors and hereditary traits, a colorful and picturesque linguistic procedure which came to be known as "putting you in the dozens." Later, this was simply called "Jiving" someone.

Subsequently, ragtime musicians picked up the term and it soon came to mean "all things to all men," it began to express many things, to describe many new things, and since 1930 Jive has been accepted as the trade-name for "swing" music, for the "jitterbug" population, and as the key to a complete new world in itself. Today, instead of bearing a connotation concerning one's parents, one's appearance, or one's knowledge, Jive, instead of being used disparagingly, as a term of opprobrium, has acquired honor, dignity—class.

2. What Is the Purpose of Jive?

Basic Jive has two main purposes—

1. To serve as an auxiliary slanguage, one that is easily and quickly learned, in which the rules of grammar and sentence construction are so simple they are practically non-existent. This "second" language can be picked up with very little effort for use in general communication and social intercourse.

2. As a means of providing a rational—or irrational if you prefer—introduction to basic American slang for those who, because of lack of time or money, find it impossible to concentrate on learning the routine principles of grammar, verb conjugation, sentence construction, etc. Jive requires very little concentration but serves to develop clarity of thought and expression for English speaking people at any stage of proficiency in the mother tongue.

The proponents of Harlem jive talk do not entertain any grandiose illusions about the importance or durability of jive. They do not hope that courses in the lingo will ever be offered at Harvard or Columbia University. Neither do they expect to learn that Mrs. Faunteen-Chauncey of the Mayfair Set addresses her English butler as "stud hoss," and was called in reply, "a sturdy ole hen." However, they do cherish some fond dreams. They hope that some day, the cats who lay that larceny in the book of many pages (dictionary) will give the jivers a break and substitute the phrase, "twister to the slammer," for the word, "key"; use the word "jive" in their definition of "slang"; and, otherwise, give notice to those hipped studs who have collared such a heavy slave to add color to the American language.

3. The Origin and Development of Jive

Jive is the product of slang parlance from all over the country from cities, hamlets and villages where Negroes meet and gather. It undergoes a certain purifying process in which extraneous expressions, such as, "kicking the gong around," "Minnie the Moocher," "Flat-foot Floogie with the floy-floy" are tried and discarded, or used and retained. Some of the expressions cannot be used in polite conversation; others have slipped into the English language and are now more or less accepted universally, and by the most severe critics as a fundamental part of the language.

Jive has been in the process of evolution from the early years following World War I. The Prohibition Era, the Gangster Period, the Age of Hardboiled, Quick-shooting Heroes, and their seductive molls contributed to it. So did the decade known as the Great Depression. All this led inevitably to the Age of the Jitterbug, a spasmodic era with a background of World War II and swing music contributing to its use and popularity.

The teacher who marked zero after little Johnny's name when he used slang terms in the class-room is no longer perturbed by the vividness of his vocabulary. In all probability she used a little Jive herself without being aware of it. For Jive, like cussing, is a language of emotion; a means of describing how one is affected by certain experiences or situations. Among those who contributed largely to the vocabulary of Jive and helped build it up to its present-day fluency, were many with little or no knowledge of formalized and classical English. The twisting of the language to suit the user has been one of the things that brought Jive to its highest development.

4. Basic Backgrounds of Jive

Perhaps the greatest attribute of the Negro is his universal mimicry; the ability to make himself understood among his own people no matter from what clime or country he may hail. This calls for pantomime and acting ability. As pointed out by Zora Neale Hurston, the eminent Negro novelist, "the Negro's universal mimicry is not so much a thing in itself as an evidence of something that permeates his entire being and that thing is drama, and emotional intensity. His (the Negro's) very words are action words. His interpretation of the English language is in terms of pictures (remember the vivid portrayal of biblical scenes in 'Green Pastures'?). One act described in terms of another. Hence, the rich metaphor and simile.

"The metaphor," she continues, "is, of course, very primitive. It is easier to illustrate than to explain, because action came before speech. Every phase of Negro life is highly dramatized. No matter how joyful or sad the case may be, there is sufficient scope for drama. Everything is acted out. Unconsciously for the most part, of course. There is an impromptu ceremony always ready for every hour of life. No little moment passes unadorned.

"Now the people with highly developed languages have words for abstract, detached ideas. But the primitive man relies on descriptive words. His terms are all tightly integrated, close-fitting. Frequently the Negro, even with abstract words in his vocabulary, not inherent to him, but transposed to his vocabulary through contact, must add action to make these words have meaning to him. The white man thinks in written language. The Negro thinks in hieroglyphics."

There might be a further explanation to the fact that the white man thinks objectively, the Negro subjectively—that is the dark skinned man throws words deep into his subconscious mind and when they come out of his mouth later the results are something startling.

"The Negro, it seems, knows so well the power, the magic, the witchery of words—not the words themselves, but the feelings evoked by the sound of certain words. The witch-doctor with his savage and barbaric costume relied on the power of words in his mysterious chants and incantations to the gods. He was a highly respected member in an African tribal community. And since civilization is only a very thin veneer over most of our sub-conscious instincts, Jive might be a reversal back to that old love of chant, or mumbo-jumbo, etc."[9]

All this has to do with a venture here into the higher and more exalted realms of Jive, where the fancy floats about as though reposing on pink edged clouds, and the senses are beguiled and hypnotized by the soothing cadence of matchless phrases and delightful rhythm. To an outsider this might sound like the most utter, complete and childish nonsense.

As pointed out by Miss Hurston, the Negro's reaction to language is an emotional, not an intellectual one. It is the sound of words, their flexibility, and the way in which they may be combined with other similar words that impresses him—not their meaning. This might be due to the fact that the subconscious mind of the Negro is much nearer the surface of his actual life and actions, than in the white man. Which would explain why the average Negro is such a complex and complicated person, with many sides and phases to his character.

5. The System—The ABC of Basic Jive

On Learning the Basic Words and Terms

It is not necessary that you have a college degree in English in order to learn and appreciate Basic Jive, nor is it required that you renounce your present conventional and introspective habits and go jitterbugging at the nearest dance hall, in order to become an adept in its use. All that is needed is a good memory plus a sense of rhythm. At the same time, it will be of great help to the student if he puts every word he learns into actual use by memorizing some simple phrase or statement at this early stage in order that he may get an idea of its ordinary use in talking and writing. Within a relatively few weeks one may develop an amazing proficiency in Jive talk.

The learning of the System of Basic Jive may be accomplished in this manner—

By familiarizing oneself with the vocabulary.
Expansion of the words in form and sense.
Special uses of the words and their application for special purposes.

6. First Steps in Jive

Names of Things

Since Jive talk came into being because of the paucity of words and inadequacy of the vocabularies of its users, it is of primary interest that we get a good working knowledge of the Jive names for things. It is also essential to understand here that really good Jive talk is also accompanied by appropriate gestures, inflections of the voice, and other aids towards making one's meaning clear.

The simplest words in Jive are those relating to things—inanimate objects, the furniture in a room, objects which can be moved, sold, bought, exchanged, all concrete and tangible objects. Once mastered, one feels that he is fairly launched on a career as a Jive linguist.

Basic Vocabulary

Are you one of those people whose mind quickly associates related objects one with the other? For example, do you associate the following automatically, coupling them up subconsciously, without any effort? boy-and-girl, door-and-knob, horse-and-wagon, subway-and-nickel, man-and-woman, pen-and-ink, pencil-and-paper, knife-and-fork. If you are, then you should make a list of the words below that naturally go together. Definitions are in italics.

Avenue—*Main Trill, Stroll*
Alarm Clock—*Chimer*
Automobile—*Gas buggy*
Bed—*Softy*
Boy—*Cat, skull*
Body—*Frame*
Coffee and doughnuts—*slops and slugs*

Corner—*Three pointer*
Cigarette—*Long white roll*
Chinese—*Riceman*
Door—*Slammer*
Dress—*Drape*
Double-decker Bus—*Avenue tank*
Ears—*Flaps*
Elderly man—*Poppa Stoppa*
Eyes—*Gims*
Face—*Pan, mug*
Fingers—*Wigglers*
Feet—*Groundpads*
Fur Coat—*Fine Fur*
Frankfurter—*Pimp-steak*
Girl—*Chick, chippie, scribe, banter*
Gun—*Bow-wow*
Hair—*Moss*
Hat—*Sky*
Hands—*Grabbers*
Head—*Conk, thinkpad, knowledge-box*
House—*Pad, crib, pile-of-stone, layout*
Indian—*Jin*
Juke-box—*Piccolo*
Jail—*House of Many Slammers*
Key—*Twister*
Knees—*Dukes, knobs, benders*
Knife—*Chib, switch*
Legs—*Gams, stems, props*
Liquor—*Lush, juice*
Magazine—*Rag*
Marijuana-Weed—*Reefer, roach, hemp, rope, tea*
Moon—*Pumpkin*
Movie—*Flicker*
Match—*Snapper*

Notebook—*Snitchpad*
Nose—*Sniffer*
Negro—*Mose, Spade, Cluck, Clink*
Newspaper—*Rag or Snitchpad*
Overcoat—*Benny*
Pants—*Pegs*
Rain—*Heavy Wet, Light Drip-drizzle*
Road—*Stroll*
Socks—*Leg sacks*
Street—*Stroll*
Suit—*Drape*
Sun—*Beaming-Bean*
Sky—*Blue*
Toes—*Wigglers*
Trill—*Stroll, street*
Trousers—*Pegs*

With the above words at your disposal, try your hand at constructing sentences employing them in place of the words you would use ordinarily. For example: Instead of saying: "I'm going home," you say: "I'm going to my pile of stone." When you reach your "pile of stone," if you didn't have a "twister to the slammer," you would naturally have to knock on the "slammer," would you not? Your "thinkpad" would instruct you to do that. And in going to your "pile of stone," your groundpads would bear your "frame" to that place. Suppose you decided to ride instead of walking, then you would take "an avenue tank." You may note from the above list of Jive names that there is a complete absence of verbs or words denoting action. But in the next phase of Jive we discuss verbs and their forms. For further reference, see the Jive lexicon in the back of this book.[12]

7. Verbal Nouns

These are the words that move and "jump," the Jive Verbs that give the language its appeal and spontaneity, that make Jive flexible.

Here we are dealing with the words which describe bodily motion, the movement of arms, legs, hands and feet. They also denote intangible action having to do with thought, comprehension, a very important phase of Jive.

We start off by naming simple acts. In the preceding portion of this chapter we discussed the name of things, we had you going home; and, instead of saying, "I am going home," you said, "I'm going to my pile of stone." "Am going" is a perfectly legitimate expression in English denoting an intention and describing an act already taking place. In Jive you would substitute the words "cop" and "trill" in place of "am going," and your statement would be: "I'm copping my trill for my pile of stone." Simple, isn't it? Even your great-aunt Hannah could understand that, couldn't she?

There are relatively few Jive verbs, since Jive is primarily a language consisting of descriptive adjectives, rather than being replete with verbs denoting action. However, the few Jive verbs to balance the enormous number of nouns, or names of things, are thrillingly competent, graphic and commanding. Two in particular are worthy of our attention. The verbs "knock" and "lay" are the basis of Jive. "Knock" in particular is found all through the process of a Jive conversation. It is one of the key words.

"Knock a nod," says the Jiver. He means going to sleep. "Knock a scoff," he says. He means, eat a meal. "Knock a broom" is found to mean a quick walk or brisk trot away from something. "Knock me down to her" means to introduce me to a young lady; "knock off a riff," in musical parlance means for a musician to play a musical break in a certain manner. "Knock a jug" means to buy a drink.

The verb "lay" is another vitally important verb in the

Jiver's vocabulary. It also denotes action. For example: "Lay some of that cash on me," says a Jiver. His statement means literally what it says. But if he says, "he was really laying it," he means someone was doing something out of the ordinary, as in a stage performance or musical program, or a well-dressed person entering a room and suddenly becoming the object of all eyes.

Here are some other important verbs—

Blow—To leave, move, run away
Broom—To walk, leave, run, stroll
Cop—To take, receive, understand, do
Dig—To understand, take, see, conceive, perceive, think, hand over
Drag—To disappoint, humiliate, upset, disillusion
Fell—To be put in prison, or durance vile
Kill—To thrill, fascinate, enthrall
Jump—To move, dance
Latch—To understand, take, perceive, think, meet
Rock—To move, dance
Rug—To dance, gambol, to frolic
Stumble—To get into trouble, misfortune, dire predicament
Stash—To lay away, hide, put down, stand, a place
Take a powder—leave, disappear
Trilly-walk—To leave, move on foot, run, flee

8. Jive Adjectives, or Words Signifying Quality

Before the names of things, or objects, as in standard English we need to know a special state or condition regarding them in order to get a clear mental picture in our minds. For example, a *blue* sky, a *soft* chair, the *hot* sun, etc. The language of Jive has plenty of such adjectives, more of which are constantly being added every day. The following list may prove helpful—

Anxious—Wonderful, excellent
Fine—All right, okay, excellent
Frantic—Great, wonderful
Groovy—To one's liking, sensational, outstanding, splendid
Mad—Fine, capable, able, talented
Mellow—State of delight, beautiful, great, wonderful
Oxford—Black, Negro
Righteous—Pleasing to the senses, glorious, pretty, beautiful, mighty
Solid—Very fine, okay, great, terrific

9. Jive Phrases, Simile and Hyperbole

As in standard English, Jive is flexible and infinitely capable of expressing phrases of rare harmonic beauty and rhythmical force. The language of the hepsters is constantly acquiring new descriptive phrases, narrative and explanatory in content, which constitute an integral and necessary part of one's equipment for gaining proficiency in talking and writing Jive. Here are a few, some of which are self-explanatory, and others of which are translated into English in italics—

Fine as wine
Mellow as a cello
Like the bear, nowhere
Playing the dozens with my uncle's cousins—*doing things wrong*
Hard as Norwegian lard—*In reality, soft. The phrase is used mainly to express perfection, i.e., "I was laying down a line of jive, hard as Norwegian lard," in which case soft, deft skill is indicated.*
I'm like the chicken, I ain't stickin'—*broke*
Dig what I'm laying down?—*understand what I'm saying?*
I'm chipper as the China Clipper and in the mood to play—*flying high and personally feeling fine*

Swimps and wice—*shrimps and rice*
Snap a snapper—*light a match*
Like the farmer and the 'tater, plant you now and dig you
later—*means, "I must go, but I'll remember you."*

10. Jive Rhyming and Meter

The language of Jive presents an unusual opportunity
for experimentation in rhymes. In fact, a lot of it is built on
rhymes, which at first hearing might be considered trite and
beneath the notice. However, Jive rhymes and couplets are
fascinating and comparatively easy to fashion. As to meter,
it is desirable that the syllables form a correct measure, but
this is not essential. All that is necessary is that the end words
rhyme; they do not necessarily need to make sense. Here are
some examples—

"Collars a broom with a solid zoom"—left in a hurry
"No lie, frog eye"
"What's your duty, Tutti-Fruitti?"
"Joe the Jiver, the Stranded Pearl-Diver"
"I'm getting a brand new frail, cause the one
I've got can't go my bail"—means getting a new girl because
    the one he has is broke and can't help him out in a pinch
"Had some whiskey, feel kind o' frisky"
"Swing and sweat with Charley Barnet"— means dance to
    Barnet's music[10]
"Are you going to the function at Tuxedo Junction?"—Tuxedo
    Junctions are places, dancehalls, candy-stores, etc., where
    hepsters gather
"My name is Billie, have you seen Willie?"—used as a greeting
    or salutation among accomplished hepcats
"Ain't it a pity, you're from Atlantic City?"—salutation
"I can't frolic, I got the colic"—I drank too much

"Let's dip and dive on this mess of jive"—Let's have some fun
"Jack, the bean is beaming, and I'm really steaming"—sun
   shining hot and I'm sweating
"I'm a solid dreamer, you're a low-down schemer"—I'm inno-
   cent, you're not
"I've got a mellow banter, a real enchanter"—I have a pretty
   girl friend
"As I was saying on the jive I was laying. I at last found the pad
   but the pickings were sad and the chippies ain't playing it
   straight; so I stretched out at eight, still looking for a mate,
   and playing the game like a lad"—Translated, this means, "I
   visited the place but the girls all said, 'No,' so I left at 8 PM
   still looking for a girl friend just like any young boy."
"I digs all jive, that's why I'm alive"
"Where did you get that drape? Your pants look like a cape"
"Let's get racy with Count Basie"
"Cut out the rootin' and tootin', and there's won't be any shootin' and bootin'"—means stop so much loud noise and you
   won't get hurt

To attain any degree of proficiency in Jive talking, one has
to keep at it. An hour a day will "boot" it your way. That's why,
dear reader, you must constantly review what has gone before,
and why you must insist on perfection before attempting ambitious steps in this hitherto uncharted division of Americana.

Soon you will be able to write letters to your friends in Jive that
no one but you and those who have a knowledge of it can understand. Soon you will be talking in such a manner that your friends
will think you have gone completely looney and belong in a strait-
jacket. But don't let that worry you. They tried to put Shakespeare
in the dog-house, and even attempted it with Edgar Allan Poe.
Now while you may not be in the league where Shakespeare and
Poe make up the battery, your day is coming, and then you'll be a
candidate for a sanitarium, but wait; don't get impatient.

We now go into the construction of simple statements in jive. It may be necessary for you to use the complete lexicon in the back of this book to aid you here, but you will find it fascinating and decidedly helpful.

11. Simple Construction of Statements in Jive

Suppose your baby (if you are a mother) should be a hepcat. As you came by to feed the little darling lying in his crib, you would croon—

"Pick up on the scoff, cherub, pick up on the double click." Wouldn't you be mortified (as well as frightened out of your wits) if your offspring retorted with this snappy comeback— "Lay it on me, ole hen. It's strictly in there, ready and righteous, and I'm gonna knock it out, but solidly."

The "scoff" or "scarf" in the above simple statement is dinner, food, meals. "Pick up" means just that in this instance; and, of course, "cherub" is baby-angel (or is your offspring something else?). The "double click" is right away; quickly, hurriedly. The baby's reply doesn't mean to spread a blanket on him. Instead, he calls you an old woman when he calls you "ole hen." That it's "strictly in there" means it is acceptable, all right, fine, excellent. "Ready and righteous" is the degree of acceptance at which he gauges your action. "Knock it out" means to eat.

Herewith are several simple statements written in ordinary English first, then translated into Jive. Study them carefully and then construct some of your own and read them aloud for cadence, harmony, and lilt—

I walked slowly to the corner where I awaited the coming of a bus.

"I trilled to the three pointer and stashed my frame on the flag spot waiting for the avenue tank."

I was standing on the corner one night very late, two or three weeks ago, when I heard a rather fanciful conversation about a girl and her boyfriend. The boy, it seems, attempted to dominate her.

"I'm stiffing the stroll on the three pointer on the late dark a deuce or tray of haircuts ago, when I latched on to this hard, mad spiel about the chippie and the cat that cracks the whip."

Suppose you went into a restaurant and asked the waiter for a glass of water. All you would say would be: "Lay a light splash of spray on me, ole man."

If you wanted to touch your best friend for a loan of two dollars you would say—
"Jack, knock me out with a brace of chollies."

If he was broke and couldn't loan you anything, he would answer—
"Jeeze, Jake, I'm a snake; my bags are slick as rat holes, and I'm really suffering with the shorts."

If you caught a trolley and didn't have change for a dollar, you would ask the motorman: "Say, Poppa Stoppa, can you crack this cholly for me? Knock it out in a few double ruffs, a few sous and brownies."

In introducing yourself to another person, presumably as adept in Jive talk as yourself, you would announce: "I'm a hip kitty from the big city, quite witty, dig my ditty?" What you said in this instance was: "I'm competent to understand completely anything you may say, or attempt to say in Jive, so it shouldn't be hard for you to see that I'm your equal."

To do away with the conjugating of verbs, which would be complicated in the extreme, most of Jive is in the present tense which strikes the ear pleasantly, and adds infinitely to its rhyming possibilities. The Jive addict experiences a sense of accomplishment and delight in being able to translate it correctly. Let's translate lesson No. 1 in jive as presented in the opening paragraph of this introduction—

If you're a hipped stud—a well-informed person

You'll latch on—you'll understand everything quickly

But if you're a homey—uninitiated

Like the bear, you just ain't nowhere—just don't fit in, since obviously the bear would be out of place in any social gathering

And ole man—my friend

Why can't you dig this hard mess?—perceive this heavy discourse

When the whole town's copping—enjoying and understanding

The mellow jive—the finest things in life

Are you going to be a square all your days?—a person completely unaware of what's going on

Ain't you gonna click your gimmers?—open your eyes

Latch on to this fine pulp I'm dropping on you—try to understand this book I've written for you

As you scoff, ace-deuce around the chiming Ben—eat three square meals daily

You dig, ole man—you understand, my friend

That from early bright to late black—early morning until late night

The cats and chippies—the boys and the girls

Are laying down (using) some fine, heavy jive—the best of the new fad

Most of it like the tree, all root—universally okay, since tree roots spread underground in many directions

Like the country road, all rut—it's in a regular groove

Like the apple, all rot—superlative of rut
Like the cheese, all rat—definition obscure, but used in the
comparative sense to add color to the series

The tendency toward rhyming, which has been noted
before, is to be found more especially among members of the
Negro theatrical and musical fraternities. These people travel
more extensively than the average Harlemites and, since they
are engaged, more or less, in work that has to do with the
lyrical and poetic, such expressions as "like the bear, I ain't
nowhere"; "like the bear's brother, Freddie, Jack I ain't ready";
"like the chicken, I ain't stickin'" (broke); "Home from Rome"
(Georgia); "Lane from Spokane" (lane is the same as home);
and innumerable others are widely used.

The inventive genius of the jiver is shown in his current
attack on the standard classics. All regard for the sanctity
of the ancient and best loved masterpieces of English prose
and poetry, is discarded completely as Harlem lexicogra-
phers busily burn the midnight oil and turn out parodies on
all subjects, religious and secular. Remember your nursery
prayer: "Now I lay me down to sleep. I pray the Lord my
soul to keep," etc.

In Harlemese it would read: "Now I stash me down to nod;
my mellow frame upon this sod. If I should cop a drill before
the early toot, I'll spiel to the Head Knock to make all things
root." In this the definitions are—

Stash—lay down
Mellow frame—the body
Cop a drill—leave quickly, disappear, or walk away, saunter,
stroll, meander, pass away, succumb, die
Early toot—morning, the next day, bright and early
Spiel—speech, prayer, supplication, discourse, soliloquy, plea
Head Knock—The Lawd!

As already noted, Hamlet, in his Soliloquy, according to the Harlemese version says: "To dig, or not to dig, that is the question; whether 'tis the proper play to eat onions and wipe the eyes (endure the trials and tribulations of the times), or to snap open one's switchblade, turn out the joint, making cats take low by much head cutting."

Whittier's "Barefoot Boy" is changed to read: "Blessings on thee, little square, barefoot cat with the unconked hair" (unstraightened hair).

The variations, parodies and innovations in jive are endless. When someone says: "She laid the twister to her slammer on me, ole man, understand, and I dug the jive straight up and down, three ways sides and flats," he means: His girl friend let him have the key to her apartment and he played her for all she was worth.

Other jivers have concocted such expressions as "Diggeth thou this jive?" "Canst thou latch on to yon fine, young hen?" (Greet, make contact with a pretty woman, 23 to 27 years old) "Woe to ye rugcutters who choppeth the carpet, maketh much dust and purchaseth not any lush!" (dancers who fail to buy wine and beer at a party).

Since its introduction to Harlem (the expression was imported from Chicago at the time of the Joe Louis-Tony Galento fight in 1939), "Gimme some skin"—which simply means shake hands with me—is almost universally understood among jive-conscious Negroes. The act of "Gimme some skin" involves some theatricals, an intricate sense of timing, plenty of gestures. For example: You are standing on the corner. You see a friend approaching. You bend your knees halfway and rock back and forth on your heels and toes with a swingy sway like the pulsing of a heartbeat. You hold your arms closely to your sides with index fingers pointing rigidly toward the sidewalk. You say to your friend as he comes up: "Whatcha know, ole man, whatcha know?" He answers: "Can't say, Jackson, (pal, buddy, etc.) whatcha know?"

You say: "Tell me something, stud-hoss, whatcha know?"

He says again: "I don't know, ole man, whatcha know?" Then he says: "Gimme some skin, ole man; gimme some of that fine skin!"

You bend your knees in a gentle sag. Your upper right arm is held close to your side, but the forearm, with the palm of the hand open, is thrust out like a motorist flagging on a left turn. You both swing around and your palms collide in a resounding whack. You both then shake your hand violently in the air as though the sting upset you. You dance in a bandy-legged stance in a semi-circle. Then in a satisfied manner of a man who has finally talked his creditor out of a ten spot, loaned a year ago, you thrust your hand in your trouser pocket—"so it won't get wet" (in order to save and preserve this token of good fellowship).

"Gimme some skin" now calls for such artistry that it is a delight to watch kids or oldsters going through the motions. In some instances, the palm is held up in the manner of a Congressman voting to adjourn, and suddenly brought forcefully to the other fellow's in a quick, staccato blow. Other variations have been added, noticeably: "Gimme some skin (hands are smacked); now gimme some nail (fingernails are rubbed lightly across each other); and gimme some fist (fists are touched); now gimme some elbow (elbows are touched or bumped); and a little shoulder (shoulders are nudged); now a little head (heads are touched ever so slightly); and now, ole man, kick me lightly with some of that fine heel (heels are kicked)." Each is then ready to buy the other a drink.

12. Jive Excursions

Back in 1924, in the prohibition era, when Jive was in the incipient stages, its early advocates described something that pleased them, whether a free dinner, a pretty girl, a new suit, or a pocket full of "easy" money as being "forte" or "forty." This term of approval was also known as "twice twenty," or "thirty-eight and two," for both of these terms added up to mean satisfaction of a situation that was distinctly "o.k." In reality, "forte" meant strong, loud, forceful. But jivers had their own way about it. Today "forty" has come through such stages as "okey doke," "well, all right then," "the last word," "killer-diller," "solid," and others, including my own, "all reet, all root, and all rote," to the "really booted," "frantic," and "foxy," terms of approbation, the dream of the perfectionist, which may be summed up in the succinct phrase of being "really in there."

"All reet" means o.k., today as last year. This phrase, like any verb phrase, has its tenses so that "all reet" is present, "all root" the past, and "all rote" the superlative.[11]

"Hepcat" or "Hipcat" indicates one who has been around, and who, as a result, knows most of the questions, and most of the answers. The fellow "with his boots on," however, is the ultimate in worldly wisdom. He knows all the answers and a few questions that have never been thought of. To the uninitiate a "hepcat" is sometimes confused with a "Swing-music" fan, but the real "hepcat" is something more than just a foot-nervous listener to hot music; he is a superior sort of individual, with real standing in his particular clan. His opinion and approval are eagerly sought by lesser members, or less knowing members of his fraternity.

At one time the term "thinkpad" in conjunction with various verbs was considered sufficient to describe various processes of mental cerebration. The term, however, has been proven inadequate. The jiver's insatiable thirst for newness and for more vivid means of expression brought forth the word "wig" to describe an individual's head, hair or brain, or contents of his skull—a word that is the twin of "cap," or its co-descriptives, "top" and "sky." To "lift the wig" does not actually imply the process of scalping, or snatching off one's false hair.

Instead it is an indication that one is suddenly "surprised," "overjoyed," or "thrilled" at something potent, unbelievably fresh, or "surprising" as to automatically "lift the wig." Similarly, to "snap the cap" means to be startled with something new or unexpected, whereas to "blow the sky" means to lose the mind, to get drunk, to be rendered unconscious.

Jive has some picturesque terms for describing the physical characteristics of the female sex. Since the most important thing about a female, in the genuine Jiver's estimate, is her age and degree of availability, the age of these dear ones figures prominently in the terms used to describe them. Most of these terms have to do with "chickens," for the Jiver persists in the notion that womenfolk come in the same category as the barnyard's feathered inhabitants. So he describes the youngest of them, the least experienced, and hence the most dangerous, if he's in California, as "San Quentin Quail," or "Wings Over Sing Sing" if you are in New York. The pretty, youthful female, aware of her charms is known as a "fine young bantam." She is in the 15 to 20 year old class. Those from 18 to 20 are designated as "fine young chicks." Between 20 and 25 they are simply "chicks." The 25 to 30 bracket takes in the "fine young hens." Between 30 and 33 they are just "fine hens," and over 35 they are plain "hens."

In rare instances, an extraordinarily handsome or desirable member of the 33 to 45 group is considered worth "broiling" or "frying." The Jiver expresses his condemnation of the female of 45 and up, who has a yen for the company of young males half her age, by designating her as a "stewer," or in some cases, just plain "harpy," which is another type of fowl that has not yet encountered a hot pan of grease, or been put to the acid test of a pot full of hot water very heavily salted.

There are also other assorted names definitely not of the barnyard variety, which befit the female in the Jiver's sight. For example, "chippie" is commonly used to designate a racy, rather slender type of girl, who is good company, who can dance expertly, who has the money to pay her own way, who has a job, or is looking for one, and whose very attitude of independence makes her desirable.

"Scribe" is another way of describing the same sort of young woman. But it carries with it a connotation of affection. A "scribe" is a young woman definitely dear to the Jiver's heart. "Saw" is more of a derogatory term. It refers to the wife, or some other nagging female, whose tongue has that sawing quality, which would arouse goose pimples along the hearer's spine, when her shrill voice is heard raised in protest against something or other.

Masculine nouns are entirely different, of course. They begin with "cat," which was a descriptive term originally used to designate a "hot" musician, improvising a number on his favorite instrument. But later this term was used to designate mankind, inclusive, all those whose imagination worked above a certain more or less ordinary mental level.

"A Square" is the poor chap who works for a living, who does not know any of the "angles," and who comes home to find his dinner eaten, or his wife seduced, by a more Knowing Cat.

A Lane is too smart for himself, in most instances, but is usually capable of being handled successfully by a smarter "Skull," the latter being on his way toward becoming the proud possessor of well-laced boots.

The Homey is on the lowest rung of the social ladder, Homey being distinctly a derogatory term, a term which is the last word in opprobrium and condemnation. The genuine "hepcat" has nothing but scorn and contempt for the "Homey." How can he be so stupid? He's a stay-at-home, he reads heavy books about the goings-on in the 14th and 15th Century, while drawing his breath in the 20th. He's distinctly a mama's boy, under the influence of feminine domination; he doesn't even know as much about life as does the unenlightened Lane, the Cat, and the Skull.

According to a Hepcat's viewpoint, both the Square and the Homey miss a great deal in life.

"The Perfect Lamb" also ranks along with The Homey, for while he's no mama's boy, he is always on the outside looking in. "The Perfect Rum" is a male who falls in this same category.

There is also, by the same attribute, The Perfect Lane. Lanes are usually referred to as having made figurative trips to "Spain," or "Fort Wayne," or "Spokane." The Square, on the other hand, is most generally to be found, "hunting for Miss St. Claire," or, "trying to be in there like the Bear."

The Homey, by popular consent in the world of Jive talk, usually evolves into the "Home from Rome."

"Jackson" in its original derivation referred to a colored fellow. (Phil Harris, please note.) While a Stud is a male of any stature, width, color, or weight.

13. Advanced Reading in Jive—Sam D. Home's Soliloquy

A Square ain't nothing but a Lane, and a Lane ain't nothing but a Rum, and a Rum ain't nothing but a Perfect Lamb; and a Perfect Lamb comes on like the Goodwill Hour—and tips away, Jackson, like the Widder Brown. If I was booted, truly booted, I'd lay a solid beg on my righteous scribe, and knock a scoff on the zoom on Turkey Day. In fact, I'd cop a trot to her frantic dommy, lay a mellow ring on the heavy buzz, give her Poppa Stoppa the groovy bend; and then lay my trill into the scoff-pad, hitch one of those most anxious lilywhites around my stretcher; cop a mellow squat and start forking. But my thinkpad is a drag, when it comes to a triple-quick-click; and that's why I'm out here eating fish-heads and scrambling for the gills, instead of being a round-tripper, good for a double-deuce of bags every play.

Every time I shoot for the side-pocket, I scratch. I hunch

the pinball layout, Jack, and it's an unhipped tilt. I'm a true Rum: A Perfect Lamb that ain't been clipped. Instead of my groundpads being spread under my bantam's heavy oak, scarfing down some solid scarf, I'm out here with Mister Hawkins, wriggling and twisting, ducking and dodging, and skulking close to the buildings; jumping to knock a stool in the greasy spoon and slice my chops on a bowl of beef and shinny beans with the deuce of demons I knocked on that last beg on the stem. Lawd! Who shall it be? Peace, Father, it's truly wonderful, or Uncle Sam Here I Come?

Picking up from the sentence following the one about the Goodwill Hour, Sam D. Home, in his soliloquy, really said—

"If I understood things and was really smart, I'd have asked my girl friend to invite me to dinner on Thanksgiving Day. In fact, right now, I'd run to her comfortable home, ring the bell, bow to her father, and walk into the dining room, where I'd put a napkin around my neck, take a seat and start eating. But my thinking is faulty when it comes to quick thinking; that is why I'm out on the street trying to promote a free dinner, instead of hitting home runs like good ballplayers do. Every time I put forth an effort, I fail to achieve my purpose. Everything I do turns out wrong. I'm really a simple fellow playing in hard luck. Instead of having my feet under my girl friend's dinner table eating a good dinner, I'm out here in the wintry gale, trying to make my way without freezing to death to the lunch wagon for a bowl of chili for 20 cents I just borrowed from somebody on the Avenue. What shall it be, Father Divine's Restaurant and Heavenly Kingdom, or do I join the United States Army?"

So contagious is the inclination to talk in this jive lingo that already certain aspects of it have and are emerging in the commercial world, in the movies, the daily comic sheets, over the radio and on popular recordings. Orson Welles, the playwright-actor, told the author one of his plays will have a jive theme. The movie hit "Second Chorus," with Fred Astaire and Artie Shaw, featured an overdose of jive talk and jive dancing, freshly imported from Harlem. Popular comic strip characters in "Terry and the Pirates" were found talking in a really "hipped" manner to escape from a dire predicament.

Some high-brow psychiatrist might say that jive is the language of the "infantile-extrovert," but be that as it may, one can wander up Harlem way, night or day; pause for a bus or a cab, and one's ears are suddenly assailed by a bombardment of "Whatcha know, ole man?" "I'm like the bear, just ain't nowhere, but here to dig for Miss St. Clair". . . "An' she laid the twister to her slammer on me, ole man, understand, and I dug the jive straight up an' down, three ways, sides and flats" . . . Or: "Gimme some skin, ole man. That's righteous, Jackson, truly reecheous. In fact, it's roacheous. I'm gonna put that right in my pocket so it won't get wet" . . . "I'm playing the dozens with my uncle's cousins; eatin' onions an' wiping my eyes" . . . "The heavy sugar I'm laying down, ole man, understand, is harder than Norwegian lard. Lay a little of that fine skin on me, stud-hoss."

Such jargon is reminiscent of Tibet, Afghanistan, as unintelligible to the uninitiate as listening to a foreign dictator's harangue over a shortwave broadcast. One is confused and bewildered over this seemingly incomprehensible idiom. You forget about taking a cab or bus, and, lured by a sense of the occult and exotic, edge in closer to hear more, completely enchanted by the scene which greets your eyes—fellows in wide-brimmed fuzzy hats, pistol-cuffed trousers with balloon-like knees and frock-like coats the length of a clergyman's; you listen in breathless fascination as they exchange verbal bombshells, rhymed and lyrical, and although you do not know it, you are listening to the new poetry of the proletariat.

You glance about you in dismay. What has happened to the Harlem you thought you knew so well, or about which you read so much? Where are the poets, the high-brow intellectuals, the doctor-writers, and musicians, who spoke Harlem's language in the days of the Black Renaissance—that period ushered in by Carl Van Vechten and his "Nigger Heaven?"[12] Harlem, apparently, has side-tracked her intellectuals. So, although you are unaware of it as yet, they have invented this picturesque new language, the language of action, which comes from the bars, the dance-halls, the prisons, honkey-tonks, gin mills, etc., wherever people are busy living, loving, fighting, working or conniving to get the better of one another.

You tap your nearest companion, a serious-looking man in the crowd, on the shoulder and ask him, "What kind of colored folk are these? What are they talking about?"

His answer is this— "They're talking the new jive language, my friend." As you listen to further parlance on the part of the zoot suiters, gradually it dawns upon you that you are listening to the essence of slang gleaned from all nations, cities, hamlets, and villages. You're listening to a purifying process in which expressions are tried and discarded, accepted or rejected, as the case may be. They are discussing politics, religion, science, war, dancing, business, love, economics, and the occult. They're talking of these things in a manner that those, orthodox in education and culture, cannot understand. This jive language may be a defense mechanism, or it may only be a method of deriving pleasure from something the uninitiated cannot understand. Little of it appears in print.

In a thousand and one places—poolrooms, night-clubs, dressing-rooms, back stage, kitchens, ballrooms, theatre lobbies, gymnasiums, jail cells, buffet flats, cafes, bars and grills—on a thousand and one street corners, when the sun shines warmly and they have a half hour to kill, creators of the new Harlemese are busily adding words and expressions to their rapidly growing vocabulary of Jive. No aerial gunner ever had more ammunition for emergency use than a jiver's repertoire when encountering his gang. Each new phrase, each rhyme is received with delight. Like copyreaders and editorial writers on newspapers, jive addicts take infinite care of their latest brain-child. They trim and polish, rearrange, revise, reshuffle and recast certain phrases until they have the best and most concise expression that can be devised. Reputations as "jivers" are eagerly sought, and advanced apostles, real masters of the jargon, are looked up to with awe and admiration by their less accomplished disciples.

FRAGMENT FROM
THE JIVE JULIUS CAESAR

ACT I, SCENE I. ROME, THE MAIN MID

Enter, a deuce of studs, Flavius and Marullus and a whole slew
of Lanes and Squares.

Flavius—Cut! Cop a trot you rugcutters,
  Knock some rock for your cribs:
  Is this Thursday night in Harlem? What? Dost
  Thou not dig, being Squares, thou shouldst not broom
  Upon a slave bright without hipping the
  World to thy hustle? Spiel, Homey, what
  Slave dost thou put down?
First Citizen—Old Man, I'm a cat that puts down
  The action on splinters when thy backsides get too cool
  In the winters.
Marullus—Listen, here, Jackson, dost thou try
  To hype the hyper? Where art thy leather sarong
  And thy incher?

Why art thou draped in thy most righteous
Of rugcutting drapery?
You, stud hoss, what is thy hustle?
Second Citizen—Truly, pops, I hate to choke
Myself with my brace of grabbers about
My stretcher, but old man,
I'm one of them Lanes that puts down the mellow
Action on the cow express, wherein 'twould be
Factual to relate that thy groundgrabbers art thereby
Kept off this hard pavement, thus
Giving thy corns a break.
Marullus—But what is thy hustle? Damn all that
Rootin' an' tootin'; hip me to the issue.
Second Citizen—A slave, old man, that, I hope, I may knock
myself out with and dodge the House of Many Slammers;
which is, indeed, poppa stoppa,
A fixer. A stud that puts the mend act on slides.
Marullus—What hustle, Rum? Thou loud and wrong
Rugcutter, what hustle?
Second Citizen—Nix, old man, don't get too hip, 'cause
You I might clip with this righteous chib; Yet, if thou per-
sisteth in being too hipped, I can fix thee so
Thou can be clipped.
Marullus—What kind of spiel is that? Clip me, thou low,
unhipped rope-head!
Second Citizen—Why, pops, stash thy groundpads in a mellow
pair of slides.
Flavius—Thou art a stud that deals in the boot action, art thou not?
Second Citizen—That's the lick, pops: all that I knock my
crumbs by is my chib: I cut not in on issues of other cats,
nor put down the action with the issues of the chicks, but
with my chib, home. I am indeed, pops,
A slipper clipper; when thy shoes runneth over, and corns
stick out like burnt acorns stuck, as 'twere, on the sides

of a ham, that's my play to move in. Old man, some fine
studs have copped a trill merrily, merrily over the hill in
slippers from my clippers.

Flavius—But why art thou not in thy pad, at thy real hustle,
wrapping reefers, this bright?
Why dost thou agitate these rugcutters on the main drag?

Second Citizen—That's the hype, home; to get these simple
studs down on their bare meat, which,
Touching yon street, wouldst knock them to the play
That they need new slides and, thus, I fall in
On the action. However, poppa stoppa, we really are out
here, hootin' and tootin' to dig that cat,
Caesar, and to jive him about the mellow action he hast put
down.

Marullus—Wherefore dost thou whoop and holler,
And thy slave thou dost not collar? What play hast he put
down?
What studs has he put the act upon to bring to Rome
To sciffle and scuffle behind his wheel-chair?
You unhipped squares, you rugcutters, you low and
ungroovy cats!
O you studs with the chimeless tick-tocks, you
Perfect Lanes and simple Rums of Rome,
Have ye never dug that cat, Pompey? Many a time
Have ye puffed your hope with righteous rope
Til thou went up like a bomber past towers and
Glass-gazers,
Your little studs in your grabbers, and there have
Copped a squat
All the mellow bright, as thou waited to see
That stud, Pompey, put down his broom on the main mid
of Rome:
And when you gimmed his wheel chair,
Have ye not beat out a solid chorus,

That Tiber did a Lindy underneath her banks,
To latch on to the hootin' and rootin'
Made in her brace o' sides?
And do you now knock thyselves out in
Thy best drapes and righteous capes?
And do you now cop a stop and close down shop?
And do you now spread the sweet-smells in his way,
That falls in all mellow and fine, over Pompey's Goo?
Cut out!
Broom to thy cribs, cop a bend on thy deuce o' dukes and
    knock a spiel to the Head
Knocks to nix out this play
That will bring the goofy-dust action down on this hard
    issue.
Flavius—Knock a trot, good hustlers, and for
    This wrong action,
Gather all the poor studs and cats like thee:
Trick 'em down to the Tiber and splatter salties
Into that winding drink till the lowest stream
Do mug the most fine banks of all.
All Lanes, Squares and Rums Nix.
Dig, when you put down the proper spiel,
They cut out without backcapping, their gumbeating is
    knocked out by their guilt.
Knock a trill down that way toward the Mighty Dome;
I'll cut out this way: Undrape them dolls,
If thou latch on to any that ain't so ain't.
Marullus—Is that our play, old man?
Flavius—I'm driving this hoss, Jackson: Let no dolls be stashed
    about with the Jive Caesar picked up upon. I'll do a little
    stooping and snooping and nix out all stray floorchoppers
    and weedheads I dig on the mid;
    And home, you dupe my action, where you dig 'em slicing
      brick

On the cruncher in front of them peppermint cribs and joy
    joints.
If we act now, old man, we can chop that cat Caesar down
To our size,
Since he has had no hemp, he can't fly too high;
Who else would blow gage all by himself
And blimp himself 'way up there on the Blue Broadway
While us poor hustlers must, perforce,
Always be ducking and dodging, slipping and sliding,
Trying to keep out of the House of Countless Slammers?

Marullus and Flavius Knock a Broom.

Portrait of a Cool Stud Hyping His Chick

Looka here, Babes, I'm too busy to spiel too long to any one hen. But I wanna put it down for you once and for all. I'm too hipped for any small beg acts and I ain't never in the mood to be so crude as to drop my gold on a chick that's bold. I'm a CI. I ain't no GI, so get on the right track and stay til I get back cause I'm a hustler, a rustler, the solid hipster they all boost, and the King of the Robber's Roost! I've put down issues and solid action for the whole world's complete satisfaction, from the Golden West to the Righteous East! I'm a cool fool, to say the least. I've got chicks and hens, fryer and broilers, bantams and pullets and some that are spoilers.

They all gotta give, for me to let 'em live! I'm the stud who wears one good boot, in the toe of which is all my loot. I'm also mean and dirty, rotten, lowdown, bad, and thirty. Yep, I went around one day to see my Uncle Sam, but that stud didn't want me because of what I am. I'm really bad, Babes. I'm rough and I'm tough. I've climbed the Rocky Mountains, fought the grizzly bear; I've trailed the wild panther to his hidden lair. I've crossed the great Sahara Desert, Babes, I've swam the Rio Grande; I fought with Pancho Villa and his blood-thirsty band.

I've robbed groceries, held up stores; broken out windows and knocked down doors. I've killed elephants and some gorillas, too; I've walked through Hell with a boot and a shoe; I use tiger teeth for toothpicks, drink lion's blood for my soup—I'm a player and a parlayer when I see a chicken coop. Only yesterday, Babes, a rattlesnake bit me, crawled away and died, and you know, Honeychile, your papa never lied! Remember last week when that cyclone and hurricane came through New York City? Well, Babes, me, your ace stud, was driving it!! So that's the kind of stud you're trying to jive. *Go get me something, chick!!*

109

Hit That Jive, Jack

I gimmed this fine green banana at half past a colored man a deuce o' dims and darks on the cutback, putting down her broom on the main track in the Big Red with the Long Green Stem. Jack, she was on, like Lena Horne. She had a mellow index; the grass steamed over her slopes like Niagara Falls in a brownie arcade. Them uprights, ole man, were with it like milk and butter—one good lamp and you stammer and stutter. Well, Home, I was keyholing this round-tripper like a cat on the peek port, when up stomps a stud with a hard skull fry like Frank never put down on 145th St. Jackson, his wig was a beaver like Bill Bailey. His trods were stashed in a deuce of slides that asked his laces about the weather. He'd just nixed out from his wheelchair, stashed by the step-off. Them treads he had on, Home, were holler drapes loud enough to wake the cats who long trilled to the Jersey Side where Old Man Mose sings "Ride, Red Ride!" Well, stud hoss, he laid down some cow like he was tipping on down to Chinatown until he was at her side. I'm doing a Tower of Pisa on the wall of the fill mill, and I dug his spiel just he way he put it down to this fine green banana. Says he—

"Looka here, Miss Woogie, don't look no further 'cause I'm your boogie. Before you get older and give me the cold shoulder, let's cop a stop here and knock a drop. I wanna spiel about the way I feel into one of them fine flaps o' yourn. I dug you on that trill play you was putting down when you were brooming into my life, sweetpea, sweeping all them other hens away. And, babes, you was on, like stewing corn. You see, Miss Rice & Gravy (it's finer than the beans you scarf in the Navy!) I'm great on all banta issues. When the action is all romantic and really quite frantic, like it is with you, I get all wild like a cat that's biled. Me 'n' you gotta see the movies, dig 'Life With Father' and I mean Fatha' Hines; we gotta knock the Defense Plant on Square's Dim. I want to put it down for your slightest whim. I'm your daddy-O, you're my baby-O, and Queen Bee, that's what she wrote!"

Well, Cholly Hoss, I'm getting ready to beat up my own skin to this stud for this righteous spiel he was putting down, when the green banana turtles and caps him with this—

"I'm trigging my wig to see if I can dig where I latched on to you before. You're singing some blues about buying me boxes—my ace Lane'll scrape you to the core. This washer, ole man, belongs to Slug, The Hammer, he just popped in here from Mobile, Alabama. He's got plenty of green, some he ain't seen, he'll toss your frame through the slammer! It must be the heat, cause you're actually beat, your garters don't hold up your socks. Now move to one side, before you have to slide into a hole in a long pine box! I'm Hype Dropping Sadie, I ain't no lady, I play 'em tree-top tall. I think you'd better hurry, or there'll be a flurry, and your drape'll be a coffin shaw!"

Well, Jackson, if your conk don't honk and your thought-box can't thunk unless you flunk, here's the snitcher on this hentrack picture—

Dictionary—Green banana: young yellow girl. Half past a colored man: 12:30 AM. Deuce o' dims and darks on the cut-back: two nights and days ago. Broom: walking. Big Red with the Long Green Stem: New York City on 7th Ave. Index: face. Grass: hair. Brownie arcade: penny shooting and amusement gallery. Uprights: legs. Lamp: look. Keyholing a round-trip-per: looking at something really beautiful, i.e. round tripper, a home run. Cat on the peek port: lookout man. Hard skull fry: heavy, shiny conk, hair-do. Wig was a beaver: shiny hair. Trods: feet. Slides: shoes. Asked his laces about the weather: turned up toes. Wheelchair: automobile. Step-off: the curb. Threads, holler drapes: suit of clothes. Cats who long ago trilled, etc.: those who are dead. Laid down the cow: laid down shoe leather. Tower of Pisa: leaning. Fillmill: tavern. Flaps: ears. Trill play: manner of walking. Banta issues: pretty girls. Defense Plant on Square Dim: Apollo Theatre Amateur Night. That's what she wrote: final, the end. Beat my own skin: applaud. Turtles: turns. Trigging my wig: cudgeling my brain. Ace Lane: husband. Washer: saloon, tavern, grill. Slammer: door, portal, entrance.[13]

Light Jiving a Diminished Seventh

Home, this is a little light gas I'm blowing about the sharp skull who put down the issue hard after the play went down at the trap. He riffed that he'd been tabbed for the "B" Brigade (be here when you go; be here when you return) and wouldn't have to latch onto the boom play on his right broad and cop a trot through the Land of Many Squints.

It was a deuce of haircuts on the backbeat of the ace moon of the mellow dim, and this skull was laying some hard ivory rattling in the House of Countless Drops on the fag end of the Main Drag of Many Tears. Now this skull was in there, Jack, he was frantic in a peanut brown and the sack draped to his brace of prayer knobs like a Tweed Boy in righteous kilts. His hideaways were slashed like cantaloupe; his broads were stacked like John, The Conqueror. He wore a mellow pair of striders, Home, and the top crossed his ticker like a poor fool crossing a Gypsy's palm with silver. His deuce of benders looked like Navy blimps, and at his ankles, Jack, those pegs made him look like Robin Hood in Harlem. His groundgrabbers, old man, rocked like Count Basie's "One O'Clock Jump," and the tens stared at his benders. His sky, which didn't come from Joe Howard (whose lids are standard), was solid and groovy like a skillet turned upside down with a turkey feather standing up in the back like a thin man on sentry detail.

Now this skull was stashed by the slammer in this wild fillmill, one finger down, the other wing waving as he put down with a spiel that made all the Fools and Mules, the Squares in Pairs, the Rums and Bums, and the Chippies Eight who were playing it late, fall back and gasp and giggle. Here's the batter the skull was spreading on the platter—

"Yeah man. I digs this kite and digs it again. I'm brought down, but can't flash it. You see I'm out West knocking my mess, busting my vest on the simple chicks and wealthy hicks. I'm in this mellow dommie where everything's got wings, understand, old man? And if you ain't got your flappers, a deuce of ruffs a stick will make you straighten up and fly right. Well, Jack, I'm coming on hard with the gum action and the fresh water trout is jumping and nibbling, trying to swim in that righteous wet I'm splashing. It gets so good that the fools are over-sporting themselves, stacking the birdwood before me like country boys piling logs. And old man, I'm snorting and losing weight every second as I get ready for my spin in altitude, if you dig what's in life you've missed! I was just getting ready to beat a square for his share and cop his chick, just that quick, when in brooms the stud with Jolly Boy. After I dug it, I know I gotta trig my wig on the quick triple-click since I've already booted these clucks that I'm on the Jersey Side of the Snatch Play and can't afford to let them case me and pick up on the action that I'm riffing on a diminished seventh that'll trick me when the house starts jumping.

"I knocks me a quick stretch and looks down on the simple chicks and wealthy hicks copping their squats on the softtops on the floor, and spiels: 'This kite boots me that my grand-uncle's lifetime playmate has cut out to a cold meat party where she's stashed in her deep six. The old hen has cut me in on her corn, Jack, and this means that I've gotta hit the lane before the rain, for the East to grab my yeast so it'll swell like righteous hell in my hideaways. Then I'll again blow West to knock my rest and play it cool with some mellow fool. But I'm suffering with the fews and need a light taste to follow my cues. Since I've been chopping so much Wrigley's for you cats, I know you gonna put it on me.

"Well, those cats came on with the gold standard like Who'd A Thought It and I tipped off like the Widder Brown who was all togged out in a solid gown. After I pops in port in the Apple, I snip out a dolly right away for the trap and when I get there, I lay down the Jolly Boy and start spreading my hype right away. My ticker, I boot 'em, is missing on the backbeats. My ground-pads are flat like rugs. My peekers ain't peeled enty more. My sniffer ain't sniffing and I feel so unnecessary because I've started to sing soprano. Well, the Davy Crocketts at the trap knock their wigs and come on the double deuce action with the F Behind. Yeah, Home, you gotta know the way Hawkins is gonna blow. I'm so hip it hurts, I'm so sharp I figure I'll cut myself on these creases. I'm out here now, Jackson, and I'm gonna make it hard for all these fools what with all these fine cluckers tracking up the turf. I'm taking everything and giving nothing. I'm strictly 1849—on the gold rush standard, and I ain't looking for Brown Abes and Buffalo Heads. Dig?"

Just about then, a brace of Hard Johns cruise in the House of Countless Drops, lamp the skull and digs his spiel. They wag their wigs and then move in. The skull starts singing "I Can't See For Looking," in a groovy mezzo-soprano. He starts humpin' an' bumpin' into chairs an' people, and slapping his groundgrabbers as flat as he can on the floor. But the Brace of Hard Johns have dug him; they had copped his spiel and knew that he was now sad as a poor chick's funeral with that Apollo play. So, off they drilled with him in the middle, and the double-deuce hen-tracks on the Jolly Boy made no difference.

To unravel the above jive (light jiving on a diminished seventh), all you remember is that—Gas means story. Trap—draft board. Broad—shoulder. Land of Many Squints—Orient. Deuce of haircuts—two weeks. Backbeat—before, heart movement. House of Countless Drops—bar and grill. Main Drag of Many Tears—126th St., where disappointment tinges the loud laughter. Tweed Boy—Scotchman in kilts.

Ticker—heart. Hideaways—pockets. Groundgrabbers—shoes, feet. Ten—toes. Benders—knees. Fillmill—tavern. Striders—trousers. Kite—letter. Deuce of ruffs—20¢. Fresh water trout—pretty girls. Birdwood—something to smoke. Jolly Boy—a kite. Trig the wig—think quickly. Jersey Side of Snatch Play—over 38 years old. Cold meat party—funeral. Deep six—grave. Corn—money. Davy Crocketts—trappers, draft board officials. Hawkins—the wind. Brown Abes and Buffalo heads—pennies and nickels. Hard Johns—FBI agents. Apollo play—putting on an act.

Ballad of the Trey of Cool Fools

A trey of Cool Fools—Were digging the rules—A dim two sevens ago; And all were booted—Right and zoot-suited—Believe me, ole man, it's so. 'Twas mellow and fine—The blackberry wine—These studs were putting away—And their conks gleamed right—All shining and bright—As they dug each other's play. Said Fool Number One: "I'm having my fun—Playing Jodie with these chicks." Said Fool Number Two: "That ain't so new—I've been hyping all the hicks." Said Fool Number Three: "You studs please dig me—I'm with the mellow action—The old hens all smile—At my righteous guile—I give 'em satisfaction." Now none of these Fools—Was up on the rules—And were ducking Uncle Sam. All were in Four-F—Since none was a chef—And all three kept up that sham.

Down at the snatch board—Each of 'em had scored—On the jive that they smoked hemp. They claimed bum tickers—From drinking bad likkers—And each came up with a limp. These studs were Cool Fools—Avoiding all schools—Since they were too hipped for that. And they dug all tabs—And ducked all nabs—As they played the game down pat. They sat there mellow—Each a sharp fellow—And gently exchanged their hypes—As men went marching—Their eyebrows arching—And beat out surly gripes. The Fools were agreed—That there was no need—For them to don the khaki. And they beat their chops—Looking out for the cops—And swore the world is wacky.

Now none of 'em saw—The badge of John Law—As he eased toward where they stood. And they laughed like hell—'cause they knew damned well—They had played it as it should. Then the Law spieled hard—"Where is your draft card,"—And the Fools were no more. Each tried to splutter—But just could mutter—Of things they didn't dig before. Now to cut this short—And not to exhort—Point of this poem is this: It won't be for long—'Fore all sing that Song—"Ole Uncle Can Never Miss." So, off to the camps—With new G.I. stamps—The Cool Fools were bundled off. In place of "roaches"—They rode in box coaches—And on beans beat out their scoff. But still the Jodies—Buy the chicks "sodies"—And as wolves, they loudly howl. And as soldier boys frown—In some far-off town—Of the murder behind that scowl!!!

Weed Me a Bit of Jive, Ole Man

Well, Home, this is the first 30 of the new double six and ole man, you'd better get on it if you want it, 'cause every stud and bloomin' bud is gonna be trilling and drilling on both sides of the main drag and on the clip side of the big moist. The cats and the bats—and I hope you dig that one about the bats—played like mad in the backbeat 12, skiffling and skuffling, trying to get under the wire. The cats not in skulked close to the buildings and ducked and dodged trying to backtrack on The Stud With Many Fingers; the bats flittered and fluttered in and out of the fill-mills, the gin-dens and the glad-pads, slicking and picking at the huskings, getting all mixed up with those fine young butterflies that wanted to flutter but could only splutter when the bats with the gats popped in port and grabbed a 4-F so they wouldn't be left.

There are some Lanes without much brains playing a hunch trying to dig their lunch. And there were some squares, who traveled in pairs, putting it down for chicks that were brown. And every stud had it in his blood to wave his bandana at each and every fine banana. And there were the Homeys, who, during the heavy heat stretch, put it down in the surf or on the turf, with those flimsy drapes and Big Apple capes, who are now shaking and quaking as Hawkins asks each and every livin', "ole man where's your benny?" And of course, there was no chance of stopping those skulls who played at pigeon-dropping. Which brings up the ripe hypes the hick chicks from the sticks dropped on the cool fools who nix all schools. Then some of the hens and fancy wrens were outslicked and well tricked by the cats who played it pat. And many there were who acted rather foxy, slipping off with their chicks for seats at the Roxy. Some played Dick Tracy trying to catch Count Basie. And many drank wines trying to dig Earl Hines.

And quite a few of the chicks got rather wacky over some solid studs wearing Uncle's khaki. And some of the frails dreamed of whales and tried to get their gravy from Uncle Sam's Navy. And there was plenty of rugging and plain jitterbugging in which the cats forgot those fancy steaks and kept on making those solid fast breaks.

There were plenty of hard riffs and frantic shifts; and the scoffings were slim when the lights got dim. And on Seventh Avenue, and ole man it's true, the cats ate fish, in fact 'twas their main dish, although some drank plenty of rum and played that deece of tripe, a brownie for the meat, and nine for the hype. Some kept very very cool, taking all lambs on some lemon pool. And a lot of studs there were to follow Lionel Hampton into the Apollo. And a whole slew of Jacks dug the big chicks in slacks, and laughed like hell cause they knew damn well the chicks needed something else for their backs. And there were kites that flew in the dim and brights, fancy letters from hype-dropping debtors. And the action was frantic, both sides of the Atlantic, while cats from the Apple made Asiatic scrapple of a lotta Japs with snappy caps. Thus, cholly hoss, for fear you'll get lost, I'll do a bit of slacking and this spiel I'm hen-tracking so until I'm able, I'll cut this cable and hope you won't off Jive in the double six of '45.

For The Completely Unbooted, this hype snitch should hip you to the main issues in the action put down in the scribe tracked on top. The first 30, of course, means January and the new double six, poppa stoppa, is 12, and consequently, a new year. The trilling and drilling means fancy stepping and walking and the main drag is 7th Ave. The clip side of the big moist is on the other side of the ocean where the shooting is going on. The bats are the creaking old crones chasing young men. Skiffling and skuffling means feverish activity, and under the wire means to score. The cats not in are those out of uniforms and the Stud With Many Fingers is J. Edgar Hoover and his FBI. Fill-mills are lush-pads and glad-pads are fun spots. Huskings means what's left. Butterflies are pretty young girls and women and the bats with the gats are "pistol packin' mamas." A fine banana is a yellow girl and the heavy heat stretch is summer. A benny is an overcoat and Hawkins is, without question, the cold winter wind. Skulls are top slicksters and pigeon dropping is playing confidence games. Scoffing means what you eat. Deece is a dime, and brownie is a cent and nine will test your arithmetic. Kites are airmail and first class letters. Hen tracking means signing your name. I hope you're no dope and copped this spiel.

A Jiver Puts Down a Spiel for Two Heavies

(PROLOGUE—The Big Educator and his friend, the Social Worker, have been on the corner for nearly a whole afternoon, enjoying the sunshine, and looking for oddities among the crowd that passes by.)

Big Educator—"I must admit Harlem is exciting. I never dreamed there was a melting pot of humanity in a community such as this."

Social Worker—"Yes. Harlem's reputation is based on its containing representatives of every race on the globe, and people of varying characteristics, habits and colors."

Big Educator—"But I can't, and probably never will, understand those particular specimens here who wear what is known as 'zoot suits.' What is in their minds anyhow that they should attempt to get so far away from the conventional pattern of mankind in general and make themselves lurid and eccentric individuals, at the risk of jeopardizing and risking the reputation of their entire race?"

Social Worker—"Ssh. Here comes one now. See his wide hat, billowing trousers which are like funnels at the cuffs? And notice how the coat contracts at his waist, and then swoops low over his hips, reaching nearly to his knees? That is what is known as a 'hepcat.' Let's call him over and talk with him a moment." Calling out to the zoot-suiter as he advances in their direction, "I say, my good fellow, will you come over here a moment?"

Sam D. Home (slightly surprised at being hailed by two strangers, but determined to be nonchalant in spite of the fact)—"I'm down with you, ole man. What's your beef? It's a solid pity you're new to the city. I'm Sam D. Home, who's never been to Rome. Gas me, Pops, 'cause I've got to trilly in a flash-dash of the chimer."

Social Worker—"This, Mr. Home, is Dr. Knowless of the University of Propositions. He is new to New York, and he was wondering about the various types of people he has seen since he has been here on his current visit. We were standing on the corner observing the pedestrians when you chanced along, and we thought you might talk to us awhile regarding your philosophy of life, your opinions, and so on."

Sam D. Home *(looks completely astonished. In fact, he is so astonished he is speechless for the moment.)*

Big Educator—"Seriously, young man, I am most anxious to learn why you wear such outlandish garb—that hat for instance, and why your shoes turn up at the toes as though they ached; why your coat has such an outlandish pattern; why the brim of your hat is so wide, the size of an open umbrella. In other words, I am curious. I want to know all about you. Do you mind?"

Sam D. Home *(recovering his poise and deciding to have a little fun for himself)*—"Listen, Poppa Stoppa. You're no pigeon-dropper, and I can dig your play from the way you lay. I'm down with this action for a deuce of ticks on the Big Ben but you'd better drop your hype on a fast break, 'cause I'm out here stiffing on the stroll, waiting for my ace-hen to trilly by with those dead Presidents she was going to weed me."

Social Worker (completely baffled)—"Thanks a lot for your information, Mr. Home. You see, I'm a social worker, I've lived and worked in Harlem for many years, and I feel that I know quite intimately the problems of the people. There is nothing that cannot be solved if one makes a fundamental approach to the moves and motives of the populace, and governs oneself by the fact that what the Negro needs is wider recognition of his abilities; greater participation in our Government, equal opportunities in education; broader representation in policy-making bureaus in Washington; and the breaking down of the color-line in industry, the armed forces, and the passing of the anti-poll tax bill."

Sam D. Home—"Ole man, that's a heavy spiel you're laying down. In fact, Stud Hoss, it's a gasser, and comes on like uncut corn. I dig you're hipped on your own hype, or you wouldn't slice your chops and put down that kind of action when I don't see your half traction."

Big Educator—"You still haven't told me about why you wear that kind of an outfit, my good man. Neither have you told me why you talk that way. In my school it is not considered good English. In fact, we have a theory that those who use such slang invariably fail to get passing marks in their courses."

Sam D. Home—"Poppa Stoppa, you're off the beam. You need to go to school. You should latch on to the play that this is the Apple. In the Apple, ole man, anything is liable to happen. A Cat may pop in port after copping his trill on the dope, and if he doesn't stumble and fall, can take a handful of peanuts and wake up in the early bright with a stack of dead presidents and a pad on the sweet lump with lights a solid blue and enough drapes to fit all his shapes."

Social Worker—"Excuse me, but Doctor, I've picked up some of this slang, and he said, 'You didn't quite understand him, and need a more liberal education in what is going on in the streets.' He says, This is New York City, where anything can happen. A man might come here riding the B&O (the Dope), and if he isn't arrested and convicted by the law, he might get a peanut stand, and, in the morning, wake up a millionaire with plenty of cash (dead presidents). He would own a big house on what is known as Sugar Hill, with lights of the right color, and a big enough wardrobe to meet all his needs."

Big Educator—"Hum-m-m! I see, I see! But young man, don't you think you injure the reputation of your race by the way you dress and your general comportment in public?"

Sam D. Home—"Pops, you still don't dig that this is the Apple, and what we put down here is all solid action. I'm booting you to the play that we young cats are in there all the way. We're all scufflers, ole man, born hustlers. We lay down our jive on the main stem and stash away the hypes you never dig. We play the game. My drape shape is a steamed dream, and I'm hipping you not to root and toot, 'cause some Square might start to boot and shoot. You dig, pops, I'm one of the boys?"

Social Worker (acting as Translator to the Professor)—"He says you still don't understand that this is New York. He says his associates believe only in action, and that the young men today are the ones who really know what it is all about. He says they take care of themselves and put forth their best efforts on the main avenues and hide away the propositions you'd never understand. He says his suit is all right for him; and that if you don't make an issue of the matter, there won't be any trouble."

Big Educator—"I didn't mean to insult him. I'm sorry, my friend. What do you and your associates think of the times? What do you think of our effort to provide better opportunities for your race? What is your attitude toward your race?"

Sam D. Home (a trifle mollified)—"Well, pops, I'm hipped you want to dig the lay on what the Squares, the Lanes and the Chicks and Chippies are putting down on this frantic hype the greys and 'fays are laying all over the spinner. Well, ole man, it's like this: You Cats who put down the heavy action don't dig us, and we don't dig you. You see, we're out here on the early beam until the late dim copping all Jive. Take me, I'm mad in this drape shape, and I know it. You don't dig me, do you? Well, I know your play, but you aren't booted to mine. Life ain't nothing, ole man, but a hunk of bread, a pad, a chick, and a jug of wine. Out here we latch on to it. And, pops, we dig ours without copping a plea."

Social Worker—"He says he understands that you want him to tell you what his associates are thinking about, and what they are doing regarding the pressure the whites are putting on all non-whites all over the world. He says you folks who are attempting to lead his race don't understand their problems at all, and they, in turn, don't understand in the least what it is you're talking about. He says his group is on the go from early morning until late at night, busily participating in the life stream of the city and nation. He says his clothes are all right with him, and make him very happy, even if you don't approve of them. Life to him, and any sensible person, means only the essentials—food, a bed, a sweetheart, and further stimulation in the form of cheap wine. He indicates that if his group is let completely alone, they will make out all right, and never ask anything from yours."

Big Educator (incensed at this lamentable lack of appreciation)— "Such an attitude! No wonder the race is going to the dogs despite our best effort to save it. This younger generation is a hopeless proposition. I think we had better leave this specimen alone. He is too difficult to understand."

Sam D. Home—"Well, pops, I dig you're gonna cut. One of these mellow brights, ole man, you'll get booted to what's hipped, and what's unglamorous. Then, pops, you'll find yourself playing the game, but by that time, you'll be rugging with Ole Man Mose Who Can't Breathe For the Whiskers 'Round His Nose."

Just Gentle Jiving

First Cat—Ole man, the pickin's is slim, an' I'm sufferin' with the shorts. Drop a cholly on me, so I can knock one of them fine scarfs, an' a chance to cut in on one of them righteous plays on the crunchin' straight.

Second Cat—Stud-hoss, I'm diggin' but ain't hit gold. I'm bouncin', but I ain't jumpin'. I'm like the clock, my hands are in hock. I'm ruggin' an' muggin' with Johnny Hudgins. You're my boy, ole man. You're the Boss, but Jackson, you're ridin' a Wooden Hoss.

First Cat—That's why Life is so Loud and Wrong. Every-time I try to dig you, you're diggin' me. All I wanna do is to be your man, that is, if you'd lay a little of that fine green on my outstretched palm. But if you duck and dodge like Johnny Hodge, I'm forced to play with Billie Holiday; and if You Ain't Right, then you know I ain't bright.

Jive Soliloquy on World Problems

"Ole man unless you dig the swing, the Apple's twirling, Jack, a deuce o'boxcars around the chimer, an' the cat that's unhipped is like the chicken, ain't stickin'. Latch on to this hard mess, stud-hoss, an' you'll dig what I'm laying down: Them bulls in the china closet across the heavy drink are knocking out the cutglass an' spoilin' the scenic effect, while the squares in their Chairs in the Mighty Dome are shootin' for the side-pocket, an' scratchin' every time.

"They're choppin' down the ol' pine-tree, Jackson, all around us, an' we're still cuttin' rug. Our Head Kicks are out there in the pitchblack tryin' to catch snipe by candle light, while all the homeys in the middle of the board are hollering an' twistin', sufferin' with the shorts, eatin' onions an' wipin' their eyes.

"They don't dig the twister to the slammer on this heavy conk number, because they lay too close to them trotters an' can't jack up the calories an' the vitamins. If the Head Kicks could play down the trotter jive, an' lay some hard larceny on uppin' the mooer, an' the fuzzy ones, an' dig the heavy rare for the greasers, we'd broom into the King's Row like the spy, before I die.

"An', ole man, we could all knock a scarf like the daring young square with the pluke in his hair, if we'd nix out the tint to real black, ace-trey scarf on the greaser from his treads to his flaps.

"Ole Man, you ain't hipped at all if you don't latch on to the stew on the fire. We're trying to lay down some righteous larceny and it's roacheous.

"There's only two kinds of larceny, stud-hoss, an' that's the hard kind, like watermelon rind, an' the soft 'n' mellow type, like Seventh Avenoo tripe!

"The jive larceny our Head Kicks are fumbling with is like the chair, stud-hoss, it ain't really there! I'm gonna trilly 'long the crunchin' straight an' knock myself to some of that fine, hard gum that my boy Count's done scratched at last. Dig yuh, Jackson."

The Night Before Christmas

'Twas the black before Yuletide, and all through the pad,

King Kong and sweet reefers were all them cats had.

Their boots were laced up to their armpits with care,

They all were hep, that St. Nick ain't nowhere.

Then out of the pitchblack, ole Santa drilled in,

Draped at the top and pegged back in the end.

His stumps were enclosed in some hard cuttin' brown,

And the glare from his fresh conk brought all the cats down.

He dropped to his benders and opened his pack,

And the glitter and the glamour drove the frantic mob back.

Then one hepster arose from the gage blowin' hot,

And said, "Hip us, Scribe Santa, just what have you got?"

Santa bared his bridgework in fanatic glee,

As he cocked his receivers to the viper's plea.

"Will you lay some sweets on me, Santa?" said he,

"To preserve the fragrance of my most righteous tea

"Or some sweet mellow music, Or some soft dim lights?

"Just wise us, Scribe Santa, Just what have you got?"

Santa jumped up and from where he stood,

He snatched up his luggage from the polished wood.

"I've got lots of things for you cats, fine and nice,

   "But the only thing you'll get from me is some fine advice.

"Now shuck all the cases, and step on a snake,

   "And never give a square an even break.

"When your jive gets low and you don't think it'll last,

   "Don't sip it and tease yourself to death, Do as I do, blast!"

With these final words, he cut through the slammer,

   And that was the last the cats dug of ole Santa.

Now my story is fine, as you cats will agree,

   And ain't no cat so hep as me.

Trilly is my play, so take it slow,

   Hit it once, Jack, all reet now let me go.

A Note from a Hipped G.9. Cat

"Dear Dan—"(Writes Sergeant William Bethel, Company B, 731st MP Battalion.)

"It is the 25th black of the fifth 30 and the blue is putting down a big damp. I was almost tabbed in the swindle as I was just drilling into my G.I. stash before terra firma decided to take a shower. Well, to get down to cases, about a deuce or tray o'sevens ago, I lamped a yodel in your scribe concerning a kite I flew to you about a deuce of 30s past. Due to the fact that, for the recent sevens, thine has really been jammin' with a heavy slave session, I have been unable to fly kites, even to several veddy salty dinners. My cuties, likewise draped in olive drab droops and in this G.I. pad, continue to cream your scribe that lays down a hard, booted riff.

"This Stud is still playing editor of the company rag, my knowledge box is still pedaling a tango after my most recent effort; usually, I have to slave several dims and blacks in my attempt to lay down a righteous spiel for my fella cruit suiters. Upon lamping our rag, these cruits, whose claim to fame is that their fleet feet are in root boots with hip tips, warble that you'n truly could be considered, lightly, stiff comp (and that's no hype-DB) for The Burley. I fail to gill this type, for can a Lane be even light comp for the Master, when the area behind his ears are yet puttin' down a light damp? We crumb-crushed your spiel about the 'Seven Skulls' just killing themselves on the gauge tip, lippin' a lone giggle stick.

"Keep it coming, Dan, and the Lanes who have earned the medal of the hep (not over black) who diggeth the digger, will be straight with a case of hoorays and crude moods. The studs here, who hail from the coco section, and a few from the place that gives with the crummy hooray, ask that I say—

'Yodel salutation and such to their loved ones and boot the Squares who miz riff with a 4-F Hype, and proceed to play Joe DeGryndeaux to watch how they lay down the leather an' tacks act.'

"Incidentally, thine plans to write a series of scribes about the different types o' non-recruited zoot suiters who put down romance hypes in the Gryndeaux role and o' the types of Goldbrickers. Some bright, after the Squares 'cross the Big Moist are booted to the fact that they can't win, and the six thirties after have flown, I hope to dash madly about, digging the iggles, tabbing all plays, spading the dirt so I can sift, analyze and reveal my findings via jibe scribe. Ole man, mid black is here, so that means I'd better pull in this kite and pedal to my G.I. pad, pull the slammer, undrape my frame, and stash it in the fays and feathers. Sowing you now, planning to dig this scribe in the next seven, is

Sergeant William Bethel."

Book of Jive Backcaps

"Weed me a weed, Jack."

"Now don't jump salty,
'cause your jive is faulty."

Signing off—
"This is your ace gumbeater
Hentracking like Gabriel Heather."

"Let's swing and sweat
with Charley Barnett."

"Let's get racy
with Count Basie."

"Gimme some skin
And then let's grin—
A twist of the wrist
And a touch of fist—
A little elbow—
It's jive, you know.
Some shoulder
Before you get older.
Some head
Before you go to bed.
A touch of the toe
And then just one more
A little shoe—
And that'll do."

"That's what I told my brother Bill." (bedtime fable)

"That's what she wrote."—final, end

"GI Jim and Tonk-playing Slim"

"Just parlaying and lightly playing."

"Well, blow my wig; dig that chick in the fancy rig!"

"The cats stashed in the cape cribs." (foxholes)

"I'm gonna slice a bit of pig, and ole man I hope you dig, cause this jive is gonna blow our wig."

Sam D. Home Lays It Down

"I feel sorta messy, just as if I'd blow my top if I didn't lay this heavy scribe on you right now. Ole man, it's been a flock of dims since I copped a righteous wink, because I'm rocked to the socks by Ole Man Mose, Who Can't Get Back from the Jersey Side, for fear the Squares and the Bears, who he latched on to for several hard begs, might snip and snipe and drop a hype; keeping him in a lather over his bag of gold.

"In other words, Jackson, I knocked the digits for a cracked cholly, and have been playing the game without any fame, living the life of the unhipped Lane as I duck and dodge the Israelites on a bender, looking for a spender, his dead Presidents to surrender! How about *that mess*, Buster Brown, *how about it*?

"Home, I'm in the mood to play, but it's a dreary day, and I've got to get together, even in rainy weather, latch on, Ole Man, latch on?

"I copped a trot to the dommy of that solid little Banter, Fuzzy-Wuzzy, but, Ole Man, she laid her gims through the peeker, dug my mug, and slapped the slammer tight as my conker conks my top.

"I then laid my trilly to the pad where The Black Venus knocks her nod, but ole man, she was out in the heavy gum tryin' to dig the Perfect Rum. So, you can dig, I'm like the Square looking for Miss St. Clair, who ain't nowhere."

135

To Our Men Sailing the Ocean Blue

I haven't given the sailors of our Navy and the valiant lads in the Merchant Marine much of a tumble in the past. I hope this line o' jive will straighten out everybody who hasn't been straightened. It's mad, ole man. It's mad.

"Dear Dan: Lace up your boots and light up your pipe,
Get all set to dig this Maritime hype.
I have been riding these drink wagons since '42
And all the Back Door jive is from cats in khaki or navy blue.
Now I've been a lot of places, and a lot I've seen,
So I'm knocking Back Door down to the Merchant Marine.
I flew you a kite when I crossed the Atlantic,
'Cause I dug some plays that were really quite frantic.
Now it's twice I've crossed the great wide Pacific,
And the drippings from my scratcher are solid prolific.

"(Man, I know the hard John with the sharp blade is ready to do a multitude of slashing if I jive too much about what goes on near the Land of Many Squints, but if he has his boots on and laced up right, he'll fall in on this mess like a darkroom light—he'll know I won't commit a slip of the lip, 'cause, Jack, I'm sailing on this unglamorous ship!!)

"Now every landlubber thinks that all seamen fall into port
With their jeans all stashed full with many a C-note.
All because a few squares shipped out and came back playing it cool,
But acting up just like an unhipped fool, flashing a roll for all the chippies to see. (They had never seen the portrait of any Dead President on green pulp but Lincoln, and Jack, they were playing like mad.)

But now—The Old Man With The Whiskers has all the clowns and teahounds, the imps and the pimps; every square with long hair, and all the sharpies with the proper papers who have been cutting those solid capers, singing: 'Things Ain't What They Used To Be.'

"Now when he cut the port bonus out,
From every cat and lane there came a loud shout;
Then while our feelings were still real low,
He took 20 percent for 'pay as you go,'
But when he cut the 100 per cent,
Every spirit in the outfit was really bent! Yet, all seamen take the good with the bad,

"But here is the play that is really mad—
"All the simple hicks who were laying their gold on those mellow chicks when they fell into port (when she finds that he can't come across heavy) will be ringing her bell and cussing like hell, when he finds his twister won't fit the slammer enty more. Then he'll hit a fillmill and cop a back table and gumbeat to himself that ancient fable: 'I shoulda got hip to that chick long ago,' so with a broken ticker, he goes to a flicker to try and trig his wig on a new play. He vows: with his dough he won't so easily part, 'cause these chicks (from the Apple) for him are too smart.

"He digs a play that he will never lose—
Goes to the NMU Hall and pays his dues;
He leaves no address, he expects no mail,
And takes a ship that's ready to sail.

"While crossing the big drink, he has plenty time to think (He is far from merry and even forgets about Jerry; Togo never enters his dome).

He's through with the Apple and is going to his chick down home,
He says: 'I thought I was hepped, I just knew I was on. I
thought all my jive was made.
She took all my gold, changed the lock while it was cold, now
I know I am just a country lad.
As for myself, Dan, I've slaved and I've raved until I nearly fell;
I've had good times and I've caught plenty hell. I've been a
pearl diver, a hash slinger too,
I can never write of all I've been through.
I finally made chef, then they gave me a seat—
I am now the guy who writes the scarf sheet.
I buy all the chow I can in every harbor. Yet, what do they call
me but 'Chief Belly Robber.'
Yeah, ole man, as you know it's been a deuce o' double sixes
since I flashed a bulb or heard my image box click,
I know all the boys back there have many a new trick.
I can't dig the Apple, I am unhep to all new plays,
'Cause I am never on the beach for very many days.
I'll help to keep 'em sailing, until the Axis gang they burn,
So my best regards for good, ole man, until I return.
So long to every guy; so long to every gal,
Your Boy and ex-photographer pal,
Thomas D. Sanford, Chief Steward, 'Somewhere at Sea'."

Under the Harlem Moon on Seventh Avenoo

In this short take, I continue my dissertation on this changing world insofar as language and custom are concerned. The Place—127th and Seventh Avenue. The Time—the present.

The cast—Two Harlem Cats, "togged down," and "ready." They haven't seen each other since the day before.

First Cat— "Whatcha say, man?"
Second Cat— "Can't say, Jack!"
First Cat— "Whatcha know, man?"
Second Cat— "I don't know, man, Whatcha know?"
First Cat— "Jack, tell me something! Whatcha know?"
Second Cat— "Man, I'm laying it! I'm knocking myself out, Jack, Whatcha know?"
First Cat— "Solid! Man, Solid! You sure layin' some hard jive. I dug a chippie on the early G, but she didn't have no fame, 'cause I was playin' the game!"
Second Cat— "What did you do, Jack? Didya lay it?"
First Cat— "Man, I collars me a broom with a solid zoom! I told her my name is Jack o' Diamond, but they call me Dirty Red!"
Second Cat— "Go on, Man, you're in there all by yourself!"
First Cat— "I told her every time I tried to bank a shot off the rail, I scratched and that she tried to play me three ways sides and flats, but I was playing her across the board!"
Second Cat— "Man, you sure were digging that jive. Whatcha know?"
First Cat— "I don't know, man. Whatcha know?"
And that, my little chickadees, is life Underneath the Harlem Moon on 7th Avenoo.

What They Say about This Book of Jive...

(FROM THE SECOND PRINTING OF DAN BURLEY'S
ORIGINAL HANDBOOK OF HARLEM JIVE)

"Dan Burley, Foremost Creator of Pure Jive"

"Although Dan Burley will grin with self-abnegation and mutter that this square is putting down a heavy hype, the truth is that he is doing more than anyone else in the country to jolt the English language into new life. As a matter of fact he is probably the most widely quoted man in America. Widely quoted by millions of people who never heard of him, not to mention the thousands who have—he is today's foremost creator of pure jive."—STANLEY FRANK, famous feature writer and columnist in Esquire Magazine

* * *

"Best I Have Ever Encountered"

"I am certainly delighted to have it (Original Handbook of Harlem Jive) and I hope to make good use of it when the time comes to deal with American slangs and argots in my projected Supplement to 'The American Language.' My files are now full of clippings from your column. Your stuff is the best of the sort that I have ever encountered."—HENRY L. MENCKEN[14]

* * *

"Complete in Every Detail"

"You can easily imagine my pleasure and joy when I dug your masterpiece. It was complete in every detail and much more than one could expect. Your book has been duly praised many times before and after its publication, but kindly let me add my praise and congratulations, along with the critics and well wishers."—Pfc. JOSEPH F. YOUNG, Somewhere in New Guinea

* * *

"It Is Roacheous, Great, A Good Deal!"

"Jim, I have been twigging my wig with your handbook and when I trilled in at the office and spread out a solid cholly and picked up on that bundle of print, I knocked a trot to my pad, first stopping off to pick up on some joys and peppermints, so I could really get my kicks falling in on the fine issues you have laid down. It's the same as a cat taking a vacation in 'Giggle Junction.' It is roacheous, great and a good deal."—BUTCH AUSTIN, One of the Boys, Harlem

* * *

"Fine Addition to Americana"

"Your Original Handbook of Harlem Jive was extremely interesting and makes a fine addition to Americana."—F. LEE BALDWIN, Grangeville, Idaho

* * *

"Book Is A Masterpiece"

"I enjoyed it immensely. You see, I can't help but admit openly that your book is a masterpiece."—Pvt. CARLETON RILEY, US Air Forces, Seymour Johnson Field, NC

* * *

"My Valued Possession!"

"It will certainly remain for a long time on my reference shelf as one of my valued possessions."—BUCKLIN MOON, author of "The Darker Brother"

* * *

"It's A Killer!"

"Dear Dan Burley: Just received my copy of your Original Handbook of Harlem Jive. Man, it's a killer. I was thrilled pink to get it. Now, old man, I'll be the most 'woke up' cat on the base."—LIONEL BOSWELL, USN, Corpus Christie, Texas

* * *

"Book Is 'Groovy'!"

"To tell you the truth, ole man, the book is really in there and it is groovy."—Pfc. WILLIE BLOUNT, Fort Huachuca, Ariz.

* * *

"Fine Like Wine!"

"I copped your masterpiece. Daddy, it was fine like California wine. I'm busting my belfry digging, swaying and rocking with glee. It's like a tree, all root! Here's my hand, Dan."—SAMMY MAYS, Philadelphia

* * *

"It Was Frantic!"

"Daddy, I dug your wild scribe stack and it grooved me, no lie-frog eye. It was that frantic."—MONTE EMANUEL, Harlem

* * *

"That Book Is Really A Gasser!"

"It floored me to my deuce of prayer knobs when I lay my lamps on that scribe about the Legend of the Seven Skulls. Old man, that book is really a gasser."—Pvt. JIMMY DUMAS, Somewhere in the South Pacific

* * *

"Greatest Book I've Ever Read"

"It's the greatest book I've ever read."—DORIS JARVIS, Lansing, Mich.

Diggeth Thou?

Contents

FOREWORD

Diggeth Thou? is the first comprehensive book on Beatnik, Bop, Cool and Jive Talk since the author's famous *Original Handbook of Harlem Jive* was issued in 1944 and subsequently sold around the world. The *Handbook* containing such classics as "The Jive St. Nicholas," "Blessings on Thee, Little Square," "Legend of the 7 Skulls," and "Jive Dictionary,"[15] has been translated into four languages, installed in the reference rooms of more than 700 city and state libraries as well as on the reference shelves of television, movie, and advertising companies.

Today, the *Handbook* still remains the only book on the meaning, usage and study of popular slang terms, most of them still in common use. *Diggeth Thou?* comes as a result of wide and constant demand for another book on the subject.[16]

The *Original Handbook* went into eight printings and sold in excess of 50,000 copies and served as the basis of the so-called Beatnik lingo now in vogue and much of the hip dialog used on many popular television and radio programs today.

Diggeth Thou? however, was designed and put together strictly as a book of off-beat humor, unduplicated on the literary market. In it are parodies and adaptations from well known fairy tales, literary classics, the Mother Goose fables and from contemporary life. To say the least, *Diggeth Thou?* is really way out! Original from beginning to end, it represents the author's tremendous grasp of what college professors call semantics as derived from the speech of what he calls the *sidewalk people*. Like the *Original Handbook, Diggeth Thou?* is an ideal gift for that serviceman or woman overseas or in camp on United States' soil. It will be welcomed by high school and college students and treasured as well by parents and grandparents who will read it many times as they lose themselves from a world of frustration and woe in one of delightfully naughty fantasy and pure, unadulterated humor— without problems!   —*Dan Burley*

INTRODUCTION

Had it not been for my darling little wife, Gladys, and our equally darling (and also little) eight-year-old daughter, D'Anne Elizabeth, I doubt that *Diggeth Thou?* would have come off the typewriter. But their daily (and nightly) reproaches and insistence that I DO IT finally paid off. And naturally, it is dedicated to them, plus my son, Pete, who on many occasions had a cold-eyed look that shamed me into arising from my couch (no headshrinker, man!) and getting to work on *Diggeth Thou?*

I want to thank my man, Melvin Cross, topflight linotypist, compositor and printer, for wholehearted cooperation into getting *Diggeth Thou?* on the book market, as well as my old friends, Dr. Eugene (Dr. Gene) Mason, the eminent dentist; schoolmate David S. Minor, smart, resourceful attorney, along with my newspaper associate Balm L. Leavell Jr., editor-publisher of Chicago's *New Crusader*, all three of whom encouraged me at every step.

—*Dan Burley*
Chicago, 1959

How a Cool Stud Jives His Chick

(WITH SOFT GUITAR ACCOMPANIMENT)

Let's hold class for the squares on how to properly jive a chick. As you should know, the whole hep population is divided into four equal parts which are, 1) Cats, 2) Chicks, 3) Squares, and 4) Skulls.

Now all the Cats are out to cop the Chicks and the Chicks and Cats are out to pare a Square and the Skulls have been long gone since early dawn! But the real deal is to latch on to a chick so a cool cat can really click. The Squares rank the play by spending their pay on the gals who claim they are pals but who give the Square's candy to some cat named Andy and who is only apt to stay when the Square gets his pay. The Skulls cop a stash and knock their cash from the lads in plaids and then they trick the chicks with a lot of talk about Cadillac cars while they cop a walk.

A real Cool Cat is hep that he has a rep and has to get going if he plans on showing the chick the jive about loving and the turtle-doving. The Chick, you may dig, may blow her wig if a lad is sad and when he visits her pad and can't talk trash and has no cash. If he's a lamb, by the name of Sam, she'll never dig his oo-bop-she-bam, even though he's on the lam!

So . . . the whole population is divided into four equal parts—Cats, Chicks, Squares and Skulls . . .

When the chick wants to go, Jim, you say no. If she wants to play, you say nay. If she insists on balling, you start squalling that you have no intention of putting her on a pension.

If she hollers cop, all you do is bop her by going up side her head with your fist hard as lead! If she still wants money, promise her some honey, don't you give, Jim, if you want to live!

A begging gal, my pal, will break you and shake you and

make you grab a bat and jab that brat! When she's begging, she's Easter egging, even if it's the Yule, she'll still be playing you for a fool.

So hold on, man, for that's your plan. In other words, don't give if you want to live. And don't loan, for all she's got is a rag and a bone and not a dime to call on the telephone!

Remember: all chicks are poor and seldom score until they dig a square with the processed hair. If she's got one, don't get mad—try your best to encourage the lad! Let HIM pay the tab; all you do is grab, man, grab!

If he takes her out, don't you get mad and loudly shout. Wait for her to come on home, for a true-loving chick just don't want to roam. Letters are fetters, just like chains, they give her pains when you dig 'em and she has to igg 'em! So, nix the mail and pass up that quail!

This is school, man, and it's according to plan. What I'm putting down just ain't for the clown. It's for the kids who wear the fancy lids. These are cool lines for the cats in wild vines. If the chick's got class, don't run out of gas, pull in close and coast, man, coast!

It's all there in the arrangement: You flat the fifths, let her dig the riffs! Few cats can meet the test when they've got just one chick in the joint as guest. They get excited and let things become ignited and the chick really rules when she's dealing with fools. You'll find yourself harried when she wants to get married. But when you say, No! and she says, So? let her spiel, McNeil!

When she says she's behind in her rent, you're a solid fool if you give up a cent. Best thing, man, is to show her a tent and she'll be a fool if she don't take the hint.

In your role as a lover, you'll soon discover that a chick is a chick no matter how slick. You'll find they're all out to get some gold and try to get in from out of that cold. They'll beg and steal and give you a cold deal just in order to knock a meal.

The kid with the lid and the proper dark glasses will soon dig which chick will go for the passes. The squares are in pairs and they buy the shares for the gals that they believe will be their pals. Let 'em! Don't you buy nothing. Not a thing! Let alone a ring. Let the squares spend their money; you stash around and steal the honey! If she gets mad, you be glad because a chick that's sore won't beg any more. And man, don't ever give her no tresses, because when she gets the hair she'll beg you for dresses. In fact, if you're cool, you'll make it a rule never to be caught with her where things can be bought! You dig, don't you McTwigg?

All you've got to remember, whether in May, June or November, is that a chick is hungry and always in need, so you play the game and never bleed. Don't ever make a sound when her steady square is hanging around. Don't whimper, man, govern your temper!

If you start some whaling, it's a sign you're failing. If you make a scene, she'll claim you're mean. So, play it dull like a real gone Skull. Get yours after awhile, just like the creepy swamp crocodile!

Barefoot Teens

(*Apologies to Whittier. Note: another version, "Blessings on Thee, Little Square," appeared in the author's* Original Handbook of Harlem Jive, *1944.*)

Blessings on thee, little teens,

Barefoot cats with hip-tight jeans;

With thy crazy, 'processed' locks

And thy way out, mixed up sox,

With thy chops so cool and tender,

Kissed by broads of neuter gender,

As Ol' Sol shines on thy bonnet,

(As thou sweat, ye howl, doggone it!)

My own drumbeat to thee is clean—

I was once a barefoot teen!

The Hype Droppers

(BEST WITH ONE BONGO)

A bunch of cool studs were chewing their cuds at Joe's Solid Rock in the middle of the block. A cool cat named Nat was whaling the drums at this hot spot in the heart of the slums. The waitress was Sue, a chick that was new, trying to make a quarter serving the juice and water. But the studs were beat and could buy no wheat, let alone any fried meat. So they all stashed there waiting for a square to dig their blab then pick up the tab.

"I'm dead for some bread," said Dirty Freddy to Lonesome Eddie.

"I'm starving for some carving of beef for a thief," spieled Hairpin Harry to Lover Boy Larry.

"I could dig a slight slice of pig, just one on a toasted bun," howled Have Mercy Mr. Percy to his first cousin, Dime a Dozen.

"Let's play it cool," said Lonesome Eddie, "let's be steady and maybe we'll be lucky and dig us a fool for some lemon pool."

"Naw, man," said Hairpin Harry whose chick they call Carry. "I'm a panther with the answer: Let's stash and maybe old Sue here will knock us some hash."

"No you won't," said Sue, the chick who was new. "On that kind of beg the sign says DON'T!"

"Well, how about that cat Nat and his band on the stand?" asked the Lover Boy about to jump for joy. "He's a rock and a real gawn roller—"

"I wouldn't buy you studs a Pepsi-Cola," said Nat the Cat with a sneer and a leer. "I want all my pals to be pretty gals!"

Just then, into the den fell a natural-born square from the soles of his pads to the burn of his hair. You could dig from his wig that he was a lamb, making his cutout from Deep Alabam.

You could pick up on his racket from the boll weevils on his jacket. On the yellow, pointed flats of the stud was caked the solid clods of good old Mississippi mud.

"This bopper is strictly a sharecropper," mumbled Dirty Freddie to his chum, Lonesome Eddie.

"He's from across the border and made to order for a few hip begs; maybe we can still get some ham and eggs," whispered Hairpin Harry to Lover Boy Larry.

"What's buzzin', cousin?" asked Dime a Dozen, going up to the cat after a glance at Nat.

"I'm a stranger looking for the Lone Ranger," said the visitor to his inquisitor. "I just got in town; you know, from Down. I don't know nobody with whom I can drink my toddy. I need some pals to show me the gals. I don't shirk work and got the money to pay for my honey."

"Jeeze, Jake, what a snake," said Have Mercy Mr. Percy to Nat the Cool Cat as the others acted like brothers of the newcomer trying to drop a hype strictly on a hummer. "That cat's got a lotta loot hidden somewhere in that ragged suit."

"Let's jive this clown into runnin' 'em around," said the Lover Boy who was from Illinois.

"Yeah, man, that's an out there plan," said Dirty Freddy to Lonesome Eddie.

"Hey, Boss, how about some sauce?" said Harry. "I'll then hip you to a chick I think you can marry."

"What's your name and claim to fame?" Dime a Dozen began to buzzin'.

"Well," said the Stranger over by the record changer, "I've got a lot of names, including James, which I shorten to Jim when I get the whim. In Harlem, I'm the A-Train. In Atlanta, they call me Sugar Cane—I mean the girls, those with the pretty curls. In Memphis I'm known as Slim, in Birmingham I'm Clem. In West Texas I'm a manhandler and a cool Panhandler. In Detroit they call me the Hip Kitty from New York City and in certain other cities in the jive-proof East, the guys and dolls call me The Beast. I'm mad and bad and you ought to be glad you aren't trying to clip me because my thinkpad would tip me to the knockout play which might make me take it in the wrong way. I came here hunting for a little fun, so why don't you cats dance to the tune of my gun?"

He pulled out his owl head all packed with lead. Turning to the hustlers, he hissed: "Now you rustlers, I've got a lotta cash, but don't a single one of you try to get rash. You think I'm a square because of my hair, but Huss, I'm really a whole lot of bear! I dig all studs who are chewing their cuds. And I don't get my kicks unless there are chicks. The only one here is this little dear, carrying her tray and looking so gay."

Said Waitress Sue, the girl that was new, "Daddy-O, I'm ready to go. This slave is a drag, in the bag for some old hag, but strictly nowhere for me, I swear. I've latched on to the hype this bunch of tripe is putting down and I agree they should all cut out of town. So, like the farmer spieled to the tater, I'll plant you cats now and dig you later. Cool?"

The Deal about Humpty Dumpty

(FOR MID-AFTERNOON DIGGING)

It was down at Lucky's famed Den of Sin
That we first dug Humpty lapping up gin.
There were chicks to his right, broads to his left,
All squeezing his chin, admiring his heft.
'Twas plain Humpty Dumpty had too much meat
For that man to stand on his own two feet.
Humpty was stacked like a thousand pound egg
On stems too skinny to support that keg!
In front of Humpty piled high on the bar
Was five thousand dollars to buy a car.
There were nine cool chicks, smart and good looking
Gathered at the scene to do some hooking.
One cute chippie—larceny in her eye
Pretty as a picture and fine as pie,
Elbowed her way through and shoved them aside
Till she was close enough to scratch his hide.
It tickled old Humpty and made him laugh
And spill the beer he was about to quaff.
She whispered that her name was Cherry Cheer
—That she was a heifer, he was a steer.
She wanted some loving, he was her man
She wanted Humpty in her frying pan.
"Hey, Daddy-O, dig me," she spieled real low,
"I'm strictly for you, I want you to know . . .
These chippies in here are playing you cool—
They say you're nothing but a big fat fool!

Diggeth Thou?

Let me hip you to a play that's for real—
Just cut out with me—I'll cook you a meal,
'Cause these chicks don't love you and never will—
They're all just praying you will pay the bill.
So pick up your money, I don't live far—
It's just a short dash by bus or by car."
She called a taxi while he paid the tab
And left the nine with their conniving gab.
But the liquor Humpty had been swilling
Had rendered the Fat One most unwilling
To turn in his chips on a night of fun
By trading nine chicks for only this one.
"Call me a cab 'cause I like lotsa chicks,
For that's the only way I get my kicks.
I liked their jiving about being plump
Now that you've conned me up here to your flat,
I believe you're trying to skin this cat!"
Said Cherry Cheer with a trace of a sneer:
"I was just trying to give you a break:
All those other broads are out on the make
And they think it's very, very funny
To make a fat cat give up his money
I thought I was helping you play it cool
Now I see you're only a big fat fool!
It's two for the money, three for the show,
Here's your Stetson, Daddy-O, go man, go!"
Humpty jumped his broom straight out of her room
Heading for the Den and booze and more sin.
The chicks were still there but the deal was slim—
With Humpty away it dragged all of 'em.
When he fell back through that tavern slammer

Dad, you shouldda dug the squeals and clamor.
"Here's our Humpty and he's back in the flesh,
Set and all ready to be our King Lech.
Bring out the whiskey, set up the beer
Our Humpty will buy it, he's such a dear!"
They knocked off the beer and all that whiskey
As Humpty Dumpty became real frisky.
You shouldda dug him lapping up that gin,
Honest, Daddy, by the half gallon tin!
As he juiced his way through quarts of the slush,
The broads stopped talking to watch Humpty lush.
They dug his wheeze and his huff and his puff
As his face got red from guzzling the stuff.
Then the buttons popped from his greasy vest
—We dug the rumble from his massive chest.
Humpty got redder than a giant shrimp
And all of a sudden, big as a blimp.
The chicks fell away, he dropped with a crash
And he dug the scramble to grab his cash.
Yep, Humpty had fallen from his stool—
Couldn't get back with the help of a mule.
Now this is the jive about his Great Fall—
And you be real hip—there wasn't a Wall.
He's bartending now in the Den of Sin
Minus his fat and he's awfully thin,
Hoping that some day he'll get fat again.
Being so skinny chicks pass him by
Looking for a fat one to call "My Guy!"

Beatniks at the Circus

(WITH 12 MUTED CADILLAC HORNS!)

When the Stud with the long white mop who handles the scratch dips his birdskin into its crow bath and puts down his scribe of many pages about the browns and beiges throughout the ages, Jim, he's got to be real cool when he puts the ink on the blink when the cool cats took over the circus.

It hopped off with a deuce of studs jiving some buds about how strong they were and their ability to provide satisfaction with any action, including platter spinners and frantic tenors, rhythms and blues and paying them dues. They were wagging and bragging, lying and sighing, cooling and fooling until one of the buds hissed through her cuds:

"If you're so great, we're sure you can rate. We've been beeping our praise for quite a few days, but listening to you two mew, we wonder if you can top, among all the others, the wonderful circus of Ringling Brothers. Can you match the lions and mules and seals in schools; come up with plenty of monks plus a couple of skunks; some tigers and bears and gorillas in pairs? You've been around here boasting and coasting and jiving and high-driving, so we wish you'd either git with it or quit it and like the pig, we hope you dig."

"What do ya know, Joe, the broads want us to put on a show," popped one stud.

"Jeez, Jake, if I ain't a snake," honked the other. "Listen, Babes. We're from way in the future. That's our address, the year '99 where everything is fine. We can match and we can latch and we hope you catch. The broad, Claude, wants to jerk us on a weak fig circus. You can sound the chimes, they're really behind the times. But to make them happy with something snappy, let's get in the shade with a real cool parade."

"Not much to work with since Annie has been gone since early this morn," said his chum, hauling out a drum. "I'll knock a roll to catch the kids on the stroll."

"And I'll flail and wail on my clarinet after I blow me a cigaret," spieled the other who just could be his brother.

"Then you chicks can cool it while we two rule it, cause we're digging all clowns, we mean, those without frowns, to march with the elephants and kangaroos and to go with the Cat That Never Mews. We'll get all the boppers to wear their gay toppers. The chicks—we want six—will do all the tricks, though some might freeze on the flying trapeze. For the fans who wants to relax, we'll have Jacquet on tenor sax. For those who might doze, we'll bring in the Prez wearing a bright red fez. We'll see that it jumps like a camel's humps. On the box we'll put Bud or perhaps another cool stud. And we'll keep Ol' Dizzy busy blowing his riffs and flatted fifths."

"Crazy, man," said the chick named Jan. "You'll knock us out without a doubt."

"And we'll have some *Creatures From the Black Lagoons* to go with the candy and balloons," wailed the other stud, the thrill of adventure in his blood.

"And we'll have all kinds of wines and some straight cats in vines," said the first after the other's bit of verse. "There'll be lots of apes wearing evening capes and a snake on the make; plenty of worms and pachyderms, squares and some mares and some barefoot boys dancing to the noise."

Then they went out to cap Ringling.

Little Joe Bop perched on the elephant with one hop, while Deuce the Goose took a tech and climbed up on the camel's neck. Four or five cats led by Victor, gave a free ride to the boa constrictor. One stud got juiced and played the flunky, to a very surprised old Brazilian monkey. The Fat Woman, in a rage got real defiant, she rode a cage and igged the giant. And they had some chicks, some real fine broads, not the kind you know are frauds. And there were freaks, some with beaks, and some others better known as geeks.

Before the parade got down the block, the squares in the windows got a big shock. A real cool One with his flit gun began to shoot at every zoot. The circus stopped dead in its tracks as though the street were full of tacks. The band goofed off when ol' Diz coughed then a brace of cools broke all the rules and punched with left and whaled with right in a Chicago good time "Kitchenette" fight.

Now Willie Cool, high on his stool, was whaling the hides from all the sides, and from his stash his gims could mash the din and rattle of the uproarious battle. With his good right grabber he beat out a jabber that sounded the studs putting it down for the pair of cool buds.

"Get hep, Shep," said one to the other (there were some who said it was his brother). "I don't think that we can wink away this crazy music stink. These cats are whaling, man, they're flailing, and I believe the mad mumble of this wild rumble will call the cops to mop these bops."

"Yeah, flashed the other" (I mean his brother). "One or two of the boys in blue will dull this lull with well-whipped heads needing white-togged meds. So, you can cop I'm for a stop, although I feel it in my blood to turn this strut into a dud. These little girls, their moss in curls, will have to stash while we cool this crazy bash. But as we leave, they'll surely grieve and swear we came here just to deceive. They'll say our claim to future frame is based on jive from fifty-five."

"Crazy, man, crazy," spieled his pal, one eye lamping a real gone gal. "They just don't dig our kind of rig since we come from yonder far-off Mars and didn't show up in our new space cars. So let us add to this confusion and help it on with more delusion. Let's hip the snake—the boa constrictor—carried by those cats named Victor. Let's make him mad enough to bite 'em, treat him rough so he will fight 'em. Pour the elephant a bucket of pop and maybe he'll shake off Little Joe Bop. Slip the giraffe a shot of juice. That's how he can shake old Deuce the Goose. Let the lion start up a great big racket and I'm sure it'll drown out the mighty Jacquet. Start a spin with some rock 'n roll then let's modulate to Nat (King) Cole. Make it wild like Geronimo with plenty of noise by Fats Domino. Play the blues by Eddie Baron and the deal with be cool like a baldy with hair on."

"Yeah," said his chum, chewing gum. "I figure the time is now ripe for us to drop our atomic hype. Look. The spell has just begun its works. Let's lay back and dig these jerks. The deal is down from pillar to post, and Jim, I dig this scene the most. Dig that cool and frantic monkey. He's really upsetting that beat-up junky. And pick up on that crazy rhino; that Mogen-David made him a wino. And, Jim, latch on to that hopped up shepherd; he thinks it's a sheep, but man, it's a leopard! And did you dig that chick with moss that thick? Killing herself cooling on a pogo stick."

Just about then they pulled the raid on this crazy bopster's parade. The studs got cool and copped their fade. They left old Boptown in a perfect panic as they played the changes to the inorganic. Now safely back in the year, '99, and stashed in a pad drinking mulberry wine, they oft recall the frantic ball, dug by thousands plus many others, when the cats capped the Ringling Brothers. The studs are planning another visit to dig the latest oobee-doo what-is-it. But that trip, man, must be deferred; the Cool School, Jim, has lost *The Bird!*

Diggeth Thou?

Like in the wheel within a wheel, this is the deal that went down in the little old town of Egypt Alabam where Mose hit a grand slam by taking the Israelites on the lam.

It was over at Cairo where old Dad Pharaoh held his court and had his sport with the chicks and hens in his fleshpot dens and horded the gold from Israelites sold. And from his heavy dreaming he awoke screaming; and without warning that early morning, he grabbed his head, kicked the chick out of bed, called his head priests from similar feasts and spieled:

"Get thee hence lest I take offense: Like I'm scribing this bill for an Israelite kill of every male who is two or under and woe to him who pulls a blunder. In my dream that made me scream I was told that Mose Bold would pop in port, jazz up my court by taking my Jews and leave no dues. Well, they'll be a race of females for I'm killing off all their males! And that will be the kingly kick—to give each of my studs an extra chick. From now until—and that's my will—and let me hear you cats applaud; every stud'll have a broad. Diggeth thou this offbeat deal, the wheel within a wheel?"

Now a woman named Jochabed, being duly wed, down in Egypt, Alabam, bore Aaron and Miriam for her Daddy-O Amram. Then, before she could count to nine on her toes, she hit a single with one named Mose. But Jochabed and Amram were sore afraid lest little Mose be snatched in a raid. So, she went down to the riverside and tried to save little Mose's hide.

She gathered herself a bundle of weed, patched it together with the greatest of speed; made it into a kind of boat; wasn't happy a bit till she saw it float. She stashed Mose in it and with a soft prayer, shoved it off with a wail of despair. And there on the bosom of the muddy Nile, little Mose was left a Mama-less chile.

It happened perchance like that following a dance, Pharaoh's daughter, with the negligee her dad bought her, led her maids of all the grades to the river to wash her clothes and thus she dug Mose. With a gleam in her eye (after wooing him with pie) Pharaoh's daughter, who had a goiter, told her maids in the Nile Everglades:

"He'll be my son that's no pun. I'll hip my paw that he's mine by law. Now my secret don't you tell, or all of you will rot in hell.

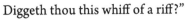

Diggeth thou this whiff of a riff?"

The maids nodded yes, as you may very well guess. So, the deal was real cool like by the old swimming pool.

So Mose grew up in Pharaoh's palace and was called an Egyptian without any malice. He bought a chariot-Cadillac and spent his loot on chili mac. He played the pads on Saturday night and jumped with the chippies til broad daylight. And when he wasn't digging their fine silhouettes, he was busy peddling filtered hemp cigarettes. And with the change from all this loot, Mose every week knocked a Brooks Brothers suit. He was a three button glutton, dost thou dig?

Thus, Mose might have died really satisfied at living such a life without a wife; one so swimming with loose women and wine right off the vine. But Jazz, this deal wasn't for real: somebody had to lead the Israel mob, so young Mose was tagged for that job.

While out tracking down a broad he'd forgotten, Mose dug some Jews like in a field of cotton; out there baling with an Arab whaling their naked backs with resounding thwacks. Mose felt sad and then got mad: he made a grab for the boss Arab. Snatching up a stick and half a housebrick, he brained that cat with the stone brickbat!

Like "I had to do it, and I believe you knew it," he hipped the Jew with a wink or two. He then drove away in his one h.p. shay. But among fools and mules there are always stools and a canary chirped as his wine he burped: "That Mose fellow, while feeling mellow, in a fit of conniption killed an Egyptian. We don't know why this was done, since Mose himself is also one."

Well, Pharaoh got sore and sent out a score of guards with marked cards to slay this offspring of "slave-spawned bastards." But Mose had fled and escaped being dead. And wandering in the desert sand, he found a nomadic band of shepherd Jews trying to make their dues peddling sheep on the hoof to be sure of a roof over their heads when they hit their beds.

Said Jethro, a sky pilot Joe: "Mose, you really oughter meet my daughter. Like she's forty upstairs and thirty-eight below; be sure and dig her before you blow." When Mose dug her he tried to hug her, but Jethro said: "Wait, Pops, drop me some loot on win place or show, or else I'll never let my Zipporah go." So Mose dragged out a king-sized roll and then and there knocked off that toll.

Well, Jazz, on with the spiel and let's see what's down with the deal. To Egypt one night Mose returned, but among his people found himself spurned. They were real happy eating high on the hog; spending their loot putting on the dog. And there was no chance the plot might thicken because Pharaoh was feeding them cats fried chicken. He fattened their bellies with various jellies, gave them cabanas and ripe bananas for their Saturday night function at Gaza Strip Junction. But this wasn't Pharaoh the First; that stud had died of his unquenchable thirst. Where the First was tough, this stud was really rough.

He called in his flunkies and hipped 'em real good: "I want Israelites toiling and hewing the wood; drawing the water and calling my hogs—I'm paying a bonus to the boss who flogs. I don't want to hear of any of 'em shirking; I want these cats busy and all of 'em working!"

Well, Pops, life from then on was strictly a drag and the Israelites decided to send up the flag. The Gent on High finally dug their squeal and hit on a hype to slip them a deal. Mose one day like while tending his sheep, was caught on Horeb, a mountain quite steep. And Jazz, all of a sudden with a great big whoosh! old Mose picked up on the burning bush.

"Dig this," he cried in a voice that boomed, "like this twig burneth but is not consumed!"

'Twas then that the Gent (you know whom I mean) let his own voice capture the scene. "Dig me, Mose, while I open thy nose: I do not doubt you know who I am; but I'm bugged by that jive in Egypt Alabam. I'm gonna make you my personal magnate to execute a real gone Israelite dragnet. From on high in my mountainous steeple, I've dug what Pharaoh's doing to my poor people. And that's some jive I'm not gonna stand— I'm starting me a rumble in Egypt land.

"I'm sending you into the Suez where I want you to wig Pharaoh to his natural fez. Then get thee in front on a sudden bunt and I'll pull your coat and let you know that's all she wrote. Now the road is rocky and hard to follow to get them cats out of that old hogwallow. They'll squeak and they're sure to squawk when you hip them to that long hard walk.

"There'll be times when sirloin they'll carve and other days when they'll damn near starve. The hot desert sun will change their complexion and make them want to take the opposite direction. There'll be rumbles and a lot of fights, but how in hell will they ever get their civil rights?

"But this is straight: they're leaving Egypt Alabam, so you go down and tell 'em I say scram. You're taking 'em into Canaan Land—for all this I've long since planned. Like in Canaan they'll pick up on milk and honey, they'll get so rich it won't be funny. Diggeth thou this wheel within a wheel, this Upstairs spiel on a brand new deal?"

"I pick up on what you're putting down, but what's gonna happen if Pharaoh should frown?" Mose asked in tones of dread, his heart as heavy as a block of lead. "And the Israelites won't move a step unless I can hip 'em to my real gone rep."

"Toss thy staff upon the sod," and Mose promptly dropped that long hot rod. There it wriggled and began to shake, and lo and behold, it was a big fat snake. "Pick it up," commanded the Voice which Mose did like since he had no choice. And then before his heart could tick, the snake snapped back into a dried old stick. Then came the deal about the hand; it turned lilywhite and then sun-tanned.

"If at last, Mose, you are convinced, go tell your folks I'm real incensed."

Now Mose himself was slow of speech and that's when Aaron began to preach. Well, Dad, back to Egypt these two cats fled and hied themselves to Pharaoh's shed. "Let's spiel to Pharaoh: Let my people go," Old Mose said with a wag of his head.

But Rameses hipped his bosses mounted on hosses to snatch the straw (which to bricks is cabbage in slaw). "Let the Israelites get their own," the wicked Rameses did intone. There was a whoop and a loud holler about this latest heavy collar and Mose's face grew dark as mud as he changed the Nile to gooey blood. The fish all died and the river stunk as the Egyptians fled the spreading funk. Then frogs like in swarms began their hopping while Mose and Aaron just kept on bopping. The very dust turned into lice, which to Pharaoh was not at all nice.

And there were bedbugs and roaches crawling which set all the populace to loud, wild bawling.

But Mose told Pharaoh, "I've just begun; sit back, Daddy and dig the fun." He brought in clouds of buzzing flies to chew their way through Pharaoh's pies. Then Mose came up with a weird rattle, like the noise from which conked all the cattle. While Rameses fumed and loudly cussed, Mose laid on Egypt a cloud of dust; and for each Arab well of oil, Mose dropped on an Egyptian a big fat boil.

He brought down hail and a forest fire which served to spark old Pharaoh's ire. A plague of locusts ate the fruit while the Israelites, meanwhile, swiped the loot. Then the sky went black like for three straight days while Pharaoh pondered his erring ways. 'Twas then that old Mose went for broke. Said Pharaoh: "Damn, Sam, this ain't no joke!" because Mose had marked for bloody slaughter each firstborn Egyptian—son, not daughter.

"Let 'em go," old Pharaoh moaned while his stricken people wept and groaned. "These cats work magic that's the most, let Mose leave with all his host."

Israel loaded up its gold and trailed behind old Mose the Bold. They hit into the desert and sang, "We Are Bound For The Promised Land." But Pharaoh had a change of heart; like he had no slaves to sell at mart. His chariots were called to order and he led them across the desert border.

In the distance far away, he dug the Israelites at the end of day. The Red Sea blocked them in the front, behind they heard the Egyptians grunt. With his back against the wall, Mose knew this was no time to stall.

"Hey, Pops," he heard the Israelites howl, "Let's call it off, throw in the towel. Our outlook now is very dim, Old Pharaoh's got us on the rim. We miss like the very dickens, that Egyptian home fried chicken. Here we are on an endless roam, a thousand miles and still not home; eating lizards and buzzard eggs, this sand is grinding our feet to pegs. Get with it Dad—Old Pharaoh's mad; return us to his gilded city—this jive out here, man, sure ain't witty!"

But Mose, in all this stress and strain, dug them squealers with high disdain. He knocked a drop like on his brace of benders and praised the Great Gent for his splendors. "I dig," he spieled, "thou owneth this field and that's why I'm here, to beg that thou reduce Pharaoh by at least one peg. These cats are scared to their aching feet; you dug them with that frightened bleat. Well, Dad, I'm back against the wall, without thy help I don't move a-tall. Just don't let this deal become just a sham, lemme beat that rap in Egypt Alabam."

A clap of thunder like old Mose heard and he dug the play this was the Word. He then threw his deuce of hookers high and a big black cloud dropped from the sky. In the rear Pharaoh huffed and puffed; that mean old stud was awfully rough. He snorted flames and his eyes flashed fire, his heart was bare, his soul full of ire—for Mose had made him like a laughingstock of other kings in the royal bloc. Mose would fry in a barbecue singe in Pharaoh's program of harsh revenge.

But the cloud fell fast like a curtain's fall, you couldn't dig Pharaoh behind that wall. The Red Sea churned and began to pound and before Israel's eyes there loomed dry ground!

"Let's move," bopped Mose in a voice toned loud, "For two is company and Pharaoh's a crowd!"

All night long in a steady shuffle, Israel crossed in a long, mad ruffle. Once they were safe on the other side, Mose copped a look, then broke and cried. For back as far as eye could dig, was Pharaoh's army looming big. Men and horses and chariots, too, plunging, cussing in all that goo. The Israelites stood there froze with fear, as Pharaoh's army drew ever near.

Then Mose jumped up and threw out his hand and the water rushed in and drowned the land! Deep down yonder under the waves, Pharaoh's army found watery graves. Well, Jazz, I've had it, this is the deal that went down in the wheel in a wheel. And Mose went on, but he blew his tam like on that trot from Egypt Alabam. Nobody knows where like he stashed his frame, but the whole world knows Mose was his name!

Mojo Digs Rojo

(WITH TWO BONGOS)

(There's no sense at all in not being hip. That's the difference between those who get that "bread" and those whose wigs are dead. I mean on the bread issue. Cool? Well, the other ink while my brace of dreamers were under blankets, I hit on this as my latest think. It's a spiel nary a cat nor chick can dig unless you boot 'em to it in front. It can be put down in hundreds of ways by those who don't want squares cutting in on their gumbeats.)

Now Mojo was digging Rojo who at the time was balling with Pojo about that hype Cojo laid on Gojo when he found out what Fojo, the cool little Ojo, was knocking to Hojo on the downbeat Sojo of the way out Zojo. When Hojo heard what Mojo was putting down on Rojo, Pojo got hipped to Cojo making a Squojo out of Gojo, and Flojo jumped salty when she heard about the Quojo that Mojo was laying down for Rojo.

Meanwhile, Pojo was in the pad with Jojo and picked up on Flojo making a wild creep on Rojo. When Pojo heard what Rojo was getting from Mojo, he fell in real crazy about the hazy Sojo Gojo was stashing in the corner for the lazy Cojo. Nobody figured on Bojo, who was a bigtime Zojo, so Wojo, who was playing it cool behind the Dojo, tipped out to hip Flojo what Pojo was going to do to Rojo.

And nobody knew about Tojo, a solid Squojo, who had been playing with Vojo and while lushing, had laid a light wink on Nojo. When Mojo found out what was really on the wig, he grabbed Tojo around his throjo and started a fast Wojo, while the Zojo was trying to cruise Flojo, and Gojo was hyping the Projo as to what the Sojo would do when he heard about Mojo dropping some Spojo on Rojo.

Diggeth Thou?

It was really a crazy Shojo all through the Nojo, and after the Plojo was picked up by Hojo and related to Flojo, the cool little Ojo, all the Pojos knew what the spiel would be when the Zojo got mixed up with the Squojo and the Sojo fell in fast on the Quojo. Now that you've picked up on this new Bojo, are you hipped to the Sojo so that your Zojo won't fall in the Spojo and the Quojo make a Squojo out of all the Pojos who would like to be Slojos while the Fojos is on with the Ojo? Of course, nobody wants to be a Squojo when it's so easy to be a Projo.

(The idea here is to figure out combinations of sounds to mean certain things and then to hip your queen or your ace as to the key words, or use the alphabet and alliterations in sounds to designate the things that took place. In this spiel above, I've told you a complete story. See if you can figure it out and boot me to what you dug with a kite jet to my stash.)

The Spider

(WITH TWO GUITARS, ONE BONGO)

(It's all in the Approach; the way one Attacks the Problem. Mary Howitt's famous Spider was out to play a hunch and dig his lunch in his prosaic manner of acquiring his daily viands. Our Modern Hepcat was out for purposes best explained herewith.—Author's Note).

"Will you trill into my dommy," spieled the beatnik to the Chick,
"'Tis the gonest little dommy that a chick like you could pick.
Like the pathway to my dommy is down yon neoned Stem,

178

I've got a real mad layout, to gas you with this dim."
"Nix-nay," said the Out There Chick, "to con me just ain't hep,
For she who trills down yon Stem must cop a damaged rep!"
"I'm hip you must be on the beam from balling through the
    night,
Will you dig my small patio?" sang the Hep One to the Sprite.
"Like there are hassocks scattered here and yon, rugs up to
    your knees,
And if you want to dig some Diz, there won't be any fees."
"O nix-nay," said the Little Broad, "for my mama told me so,
'Don't ever let one cruise you in just to hear 'em blow'."
"Then," said the real Cool Cat, "Look—I dig you the most,
Why don't you let me prove it that I'm the perfect host?
I have within my comfy shed bottles of rare red wine,
And lots of sides and tapes of sounds, I'm sure you'll find
    divine."
"Like O tab it," said the Sugar Chile, "My name is Chili Mac,
I dig the play about your cave—the password there is *smack!*"
"Cool Lady," purred the Hep Chap, "You're mad to be so slick,
I dig your well-stacked drumsticks—they make me nervous,
    Chick!
I've got a wall of etchings, with lines as sharp as dirks,
So modulate to my flat where you can dig the works."
"O nix-nay," said the Cautious Chick, "My Ma would never dig,
Her only daughter in a pad—she'd blow her natural wig!"
The Beatnik knocked his stroll right then, went straight down
    to his dom,
For long ago he'd dug the riff the broad would cross her mom:
So, he set his trap and baited it—the best he has on wax,
Set out his wine, turned down the lights, put on his newest
    slacks.
He then hit stone (the Stem, I mean) and softly beat his spiel:
"Hey Queen, come here to me—you real fine noontime meal!"
Well, man, let's face it, these chicks today are wild,

They pick up on each bopster's hype just like a simple child.
The magic words are countless, but each one means, "please
    give—
I must have loot, a car, a mink, to get along and live."
While this one was Zsa Zsa, she knew her chorus right,
And just like Yardbird Parker, would solo on her flight.
So, when the Hepcat sounded her, she was bound to beat him
    down,
Like others in her life of play, he was just another clown.
So after he had sounded and she had dug his riff,
She cut into his dommy and helped him kill the fifth.
When he figured she was stoning (the red wine's potent spell);
He started in to whistling "The Farmer in the Dell."
He laid his claws upon her, like to caress her snoring shape,
"O nix-nay," said this Real Hep Broad, "I don't conk out on
    grape!
I've listened to my Mama—dug all her spiels 'bout sips:
'Darling,' she once told me, 'You try to crack the whips;
Let the cats who'd cruise you, first put it in thy purse,
Heed no talk of the future when they say they'll reimburse.'
So you jived me into your dommy, this really frantic pad,
A place for dull repentance for those who would be bad;
You're crazy man, real crazy, if you should dare to think,
That I've become so trusting to leave without a mink;
The bulls are outside like prowling, around in white-topped cars,
All I need do is holler to draw a flock of stars.
"Here's a deal on your dommy—Let's share it, just we two;
I'm single and ambitious and could stand some help from you.
Let's dig us up a Sky Man who'll tie the knot for us—
And I will shake your shoulder—you make that morning bus."
So, the Beatnik by now was transformed—a homo sapiens rare
The Slick Kid clipped by Genius, a plain, four-cornered Square.

Adventure of Little Louie Hopp

(SANDALS WILL HELP KEEP YOU HIGH)

With a pocketful of green I was digging the scene the other bright within sound and sight of Little Louie Hopp who was tied to a cop. Since I knew Louie and that he deals in "chop suey," like I was plotting a sham behind which I could scram, when with a broad stare of despair, Little Louie hollered: "Look, Bo, there's a cat I know.

"Hey, Dad," he said as I mashed my bread, "I know this looks bad, I know real sad, but that's why I'm glad. You see, this bull is pawing my wool, holding my thread while I play dead. Like I ain't for this kick since it hashes my trick. I weeded him a saw but he jumps back, hollering, 'naw, naw!' I pulled him a star, but he called the prowl car. So, Dad, you dig, I'm behind the pig and can't gim his wig!"

(*Before my glims could blink, Little Louie flew me a wink. I dug from his mug that the bull was a bug, a red ripe square with a part in his hair.*)

But down with his spiel and capping his reel, the bull looked strange, but came up with this change in tempo or pace, like he was cool with his ace.

"Look, Dad, old lad, I'm running him in; he offered me a fin. He began to wheedle when I copped his needle and he jumped way out when I crashed his layout. He offered me the ball if I let him make a call. But I dug his stall and let him drop for the fall. He says he's a cool stud and not out for blood and that you're his bosom bud; that when you were in school you wound up his spool; that you're the same mister who went for his sister; like you'll go his bail if I take him to jail; that he's no junky, he's really your flunky; that you'll agree he once sat on your knee; that if I let him go, he'll flee from all snow. What is the smut on this here mutt?"

181

Now I didn't want to ham by taking it on the lam; neither did I want Little Louie Hopp to use me for a prop while he put down his drop on this very cop. You see, I'm legit and never was a mitt for a fake or a quack or a shake or a stack. I'm never hazy when a deal is crazy; while I cope all the strife you find in life and am hip to the trick when a chick needs a fix, I really whale for my mail. But I make like a snail when I hear the word jail. And I'll never get remorse for riding on that "horse;" and the hemp makes me limp and I'm ready to go when the cat hollers snow. Like I'm not lame in the brain from a snort of cocaine.

In my daily ration there is no passion for the rope without hope. I won't raise my roof from a ball that's goof. I've followed funeral coaches filled with cats who smoked the roaches. On the high seas I've dug sailors who ashore were real cool "tailors," down with the sewing although it was not snowing; and at this late juncture, I'll never let them puncture my righteous veins for the injection of those grains. Like I dig all winos and the "There-He-Goes;" I'm hip to all the shorties and all the two-for-forties; I pick up on rums and the stumblebums, the ones who guzzle booze to beat the weary blues. I understand lushies and the ones who are known as mushies, and I seldom have any fear of the ones who swig the beer. If I have a bum ticker, you can bet it comes from liquor. Me and scotch? Just you watch!

(*Jim, I'm not preaching, I'm on with teaching! If his broad's a coker, a square might some day choke her; so ride with the tide, Hoss, so you can be Boss.*)

Well, Louie was still gassing as the time was fleetly passing, while the cop stood pat with his paw on his gat and a hand on Louie's neckband. He had buzzed the gong and it wouldn't be long before the car with the star and its siren never tiring, played Hallowe'en at the scene.

"Well, Dad," and he looked real sad. "Please drop in my pad and knock my main Jane, a squealer named Aurelia, to the smell of how I fell. Hip the chick to get real slick and to cut for the turf for all she's worth so she can get some bread to pay for the shed. Like tell her this stud in blue has me tight as glue and I'm giving up the stable because I won't be able to budge that judge when he flips the pages to find out the wages of peddling and meddling in the Land of High where your roof hits the sky. When he digs his Book of Many Years, he'll lay them twelves on me without tears. Trig her wig that I was BIG in my fat days when I dug all the plays and planted all the lays and dreamed and schemed in countless ways.

"Oil her think-thatch with the wig-wag that my broad, Mag, was a mighty old hag, but without a doubt, I put her out to make room for my new Sh-Boom, the brand new squealer, the chick called Aurelia. Hip her, Dad, to the exact fact that she sent her bud, Peter The Rabbit, to put me on the habit; that I know it because we both show it. You can also beat it out to her that I'm going where they want plenty hoeing and where they're never bothered when it's snowing; she'll latch on to that, catch on?

"Tell her I'll be making small ones out of the big ones while the wardens keep me covered with their guns. Tell her that although it's real dirty, she can dig me every thirty. Above all, tell her that I love her and that I'll be thinking of her, and for her not to get frisky and give some other cat my whiskey.

"I bought a brand new pair of slippers, like tell her they're not for any Jack the Rippers she may hope may come with dippers full of loot and fruit and candy so they can be her Handy Andy. Tell her I'm thinking, blinking and winking so much I'm stinking. That if she's true, there's nothing I won't do, but if she's wild, like she'll be a sorry child, for *I'll butt and I'll cut, I'll be a brute and I'll shoot; I'll whale and flail and run her and gun her from the end of time to the other. Dig me, brother?*"

Fable of the Fiend

(BLACK BEFORE XMAS, MAN!)

'Twas THE COOL before Yule and all through the pilt
The cats were jumping and charged to the hilt.
The roots were sparkling, the room solid black,
The spielers were shucking some hard jive from back;
And some used toothpicks to save their thumbs,
For the stuff burned short, smoked up in their gums;
'Twas a black to remember, this cool before Yule,
When each cat was playing the other for a fool.
The blasting was crazy, as witnesses recalled
And the chippies were frantic and everyone balled.
The joint was real crazy with beboppers wild,
Tammed and jammed and dark-glasses styled.
They were standing and sitting and some of 'em leaned,
As Little Joe recited the Fable of the Fiend.
"HE WAS COOL and righteous and sorta oolya-koo
And frantic and crazy with some ish-mah-lay-moo;
He never was known to give a poor square a break;
But always put his foot on the neck of a snake;
He loved quite a few and jived all the others,
He played it alone since he had no brothers;
And he rolled his own, since he planted the stuff;
And the waste that was left, he turned into snuff;
As he stashed at the bar and sipped up some juice,
He fell for a chick who knocked him for a deuce;
He was awfully cool and crazy as all hell,
As he let the chick beat him for jive that don't jell.

He started in dreaming of 'Just Molly and Me,'
A pad on the Island with the kid on his knee;

Diggeth Thou?

He'd put down the scratch, fade out on the charge,
Draw jobless insurance as unemployed-at-large;
The chick would be the first to hunt up a job,
He'd find her some Johns with whom to hobnob;

She would learn how to lush and drink up the scotch,
As he stashed on the corner and kept a close watch;
He had it down cool, the method he'd work
To earn for himself the designation, 'jerk!'
But the chick was too hipped and dug from the jump,
The cat wanted to play her for a solid chump;
So she kept her chops shut, her blinkers real wide
And schemed out a way to take him for a ride.

Two nights before Xmas, the cat was dead broke
And was cracking his whip and applying his yoke;
His chippies all trembled and hit for the block,
Some to the avenues, others to the dock;
They were banging on windows by twos and by fours,
Stashing in the hallways and deserted doors;
But the chick we're concerned with, was not for the cause,
And hunted and hunted til she found Santa Claus.

'Now listen, St. Nick,' she spieled to Kris Kringle,
'I need something green and something to jingle;
By taking my hundreds and dropping me a fin;
I want you to help me in the best way you can,
To jive this cat's Christmas to a Custer's Last Stand.'
Now St. Nick was crazy and foxy and great,
And right then and there he made an Xmas Eve date,
To trick the whip-cracker so he'd never forget,
You don't mistreat the chippies you so recently met.

'TWAS THE DIM before Nicktide and all through the pad,
You could dig them cats waiting and praying like mad;

185

At half Past the Jasper, St. Nick drilled in—
His vines a red blaze and his stomps in cool skin;
And his jeans were floppy, his skim pork-pied,
And from that wild glitter the cats and chicks shied;
'I'm strictly for the Vaunce,' the elderly stud spieled,
And onto the floor his mighty sled wheeled;
He passed out chocolate and packages of rice,

Of the bright red wine he let the cats drink twice;
He handed out trombones and saxophones wild
As into the stockings the presents he piled;
But he held back the prize until the very last,
And angled his play to fit the lead in the cast.

THE CAT STOOD jittery, his hopes all aglow,
For the present that would make him a real handsome
   Joe.
But Old Santa was solid and down with it, Jack,
And he handed him a polecat from his bulging sack;
The odor was terrific and as everybody fled,
Old Santa cut out on his cool, wonderful sled.

Now this is the true story of that Merry Yule,
That proves you can't prosper by breaking the rule;
And try to do others for what you can grab,
And eat up and drink up without paying your tab!"

The Round Clown

(FOR MIDNIGHT READING)

Let me wig you to the deal that went down when the Round Clown tried to click with the Slick Chick from New Brunswick one dim on the stem at a sin den on the Avenue of Frantic Men. Now the pilch was rocking and the chime was tocking 'way past the Little Man on the ace stop of the slow spin top. And the pad was leaping and there was a lot of creeping as the chicks and cats dug the sharps and flats while the beat was real crazy, so cool and lazy on the jock's box in the front playpen of the trey of cribs where the really hipped dug Her Nibs, Miss Beulah Gibbs.

And the Head Hen was spieling, "say when" as she held court over a quart of port. And there were some mad lads in frantic plaids, and the squares were in pairs and sitting in the chairs; and a broad named Maude was laying a spiel on a cat named Claude.

And some cool boppers had doffed their toppers and were stashing around and digging the sound of Brubeck direct, and Diz the Whiz, and The Bird as through his alto he purred. And some were playing hunches trying to dig their lunches. And some got high, but nevertheless were dry while others were coughing as still others were scoffing at the grease bar in the rear car where you could blow your wig over the pad of a pig the Head Hen was dealing for an ace plus ten.

Well, the Slick Chick from New Brunswick was on for some playing and her gims were straying hither and yon and a bit beyond when she dug the Round Clown just as he sat down on a tall one with four gams and spotted his clams on the pinewood spread that is not a bed.

But pound for pound, the Clown was too round for this Slick Chick to pick as a playmate to trick. So she swung her map toward another chap (one in jeans, the brightest of greens), and in her spieling, asked how he was feeling, and weren't them sounds insane and if he had a grain (you dig, McSwif?) for her steady main, The Cat with the Lame Brain.

However, the Round Clown had dug the sound of the chick's horn and figured it straight corn as sure as he was born. So he played a scheme he knocked on a dream to open her nose before she froze.

To draw a crowd he talked out loud and said, "I'm down for some action cause I'm the main attraction. I nail a ball when I make a phone call. I'm the coolest of studs when it comes to duds. I'm loaded with loot, and most of the chicks claim I'm a brute. But a brute that's sweet when it's a chick that's neat. I wear my slacks in my Cadillacs, you see I've got five and that's no jive. And I never go swimming without a flock of my women standing on the beach all ready to screech when I put down my jive at a quarter past five. I'm called a camel without a hump, cause Babe, I dug you from the jump. I'm Jap from the flap on this fingersnap."

Just to prove that she was strictly groove and no broad putting down a fraud, the Slick Chick was quick with this backcap click:

"I'm cosmic, I mean, high octane, with or without a sniff of grain. I don't need wine, you see I drink brine and when I fish I don't use a line. I'd never hug a simple mug. When you popped through the slammer, I dug you were from Alabama. I lamped your suit, a '42 zoot. Like a square at the country fair, you're playing jacks while I spiel facts. You're a rude dude, too crude to be lewd and you need to be shoed. Get some boots with laces so you can go places. You make like a Dark Gable but you can't dig my fable. My name is Mable and I'm always able to set my own table. You sound off about swimming with a whole flock of women. I never dug a fool in a swimming pool and you'd have to whale a lot of preaching to get any broads to screeching over that figure that couldn't possibly be bigger without being a tank in the ten ton rank. My blood stud is a Commando and makes the rounds with Brando. And you should dig his changes when he hits the upper ranges. He's rough like Marciano when he whales this old piano. He cuts and butts all simple mutts. He likes to wrestle—alligators and bears and he has a reputation for being bad for squares. You have your toddy if you don't bug everybody. So drink your Sneaky Pete and then hit the street cause I'm cool like the dawn and really gone!"

THE COLLEGE OF COOL KNOWLEDGE (The Reel On This Spiel): Let me tell you about the incident that took place when a very fat chap attempted to date with a smart girl from any big town one night on the main street at a good time apartment in the honky-tonk district. The place was a scene of gayety and the clock was moving past one o'clock. The joint was jumping, as Fats Waller used to say, and there was a lot of pairing off of the guys and dolls as they listened to the music served with a good, danceable beat from the record player in the front room of the three room apartment where the more sophisticated listened to LP records. Some were quietly trying to borrow money from other guests while some became intoxicated as others smoked "charge" or ate pigs feet in the kitchen at $1.10 apiece. Well, the smart girl saw the fat chap as he sat on a chair and spread some money on a table. But he was too fat for her and she began conversing with another man and asked if he had any dope for her boy friend. But the fat chap, believing she was deliberately ignoring him, began bragging. To open her nose was to make her fall for him. The "ball" he "nailed" was $5 worth of phone calls. Being Jap from the flap on this fingersnap, means being aware of, in the know. High octane means spirited, classy. Brine means beer. Blood stud is boy friend. Changes in the upper ranges means how he makes love.

Deuce the Goose

(HIDE THE JUICE, BRUCE)

To be really hip and without a slip, you gotta stay cool, for as
a rule, you'll never dig a mule in a swimming pool. Latch on?
I've been around and I have dug how really crude the rude
clowns sound. And the squares usually travel in pairs while
the practical Lanes seldom carry canes. Which brings up the
mad lads in the gay plaids keeping up with the wayout fads.
And if you've never picked up on Boppers wearing tall toppers, your peepers are dead sleepers and your gims have the
dims. Latch on?

NOW DEUCE, THE GOOSE, was on the loose, trying to tail
a Frail on the Lonesome Trail. And the Frail was named Stella,
a fraud Cinderella, out trying to trick any citified Hick, making
with that hype to fry up some tripe in the rain without his
umbrella. Now her spiel for a meal was a crazy good deal, some
oolya-fram like that cat named Sam, as Stella put down her beg.
And Deuce, The Goose, who was on the loose, knew she was
pulling his leg—the one with the peg—and was playing her
hunch to collar a free lunch, so he beat her to the punch—
    "Now you crazy little jiver, you real cool conniver, I'm tops
in this town and hip to what's going down. And I want you
to know that I deal in snow and there are few who can dig
my play, which the lads in plaids call rather gay. The bulls are
the bears and don't know the lairs where the snitches get the
stitches and the kites are cool flights and those with a limp
get a snort of the hemp and the goof brings a poof, and a huff
and a puff of the real gone stuff brings decisions and visions,
and the plague makes one vague as the grain from Fort Wayne
overcomes any pain found in Memory Lane!

"Now I'm not an Astor, but I'm still the Master of the plays that come and go; and Babe, before I blow I want you to know my story from the days back then, when you could beg a fin and parlay it to ten. My name is really Freddy, but I'm always ready to have a little fun with a frantic honey bun, providing the deal is wild, for I like it understood and it really should, that I never pick up on a child.

"I take no chances, doll, on missing the dances where the crop is all bop and the broads ain't frauds or silly Maudes and the cats a variety of Claudes. Now I'm in a hurry and don't want to worry on a hype that's not going to jell; and I'm under a shuck trying to change my luck and you know I'm waiting for the bell.

"So, what's your story, Miss Morning Glory, hip me before I broom, 'cause I'm in the middle trying to pick out a riddle, I'm really on the zoom!"

With her thinkbox clicking, her calculations ticking, the Frail delivered his mail. Said she to he with a snicker, McGhee, "I've heard your spiel before. In the days of old when knights were bold and hypes had not been invented; they tightened their wigs with poppy bush twigs and broomed along well contented. I dig your howl about the bulls on the prowl and confess it sounds real cool; but my jolly good fellow, you're a bit too mellow and your spiel sounds like you're a stool. If you got a stitch, your wig would twitch, and a flight for you'd be rather light. You're really dead game trying to frame a dame who is really a bad lad's moll.

"You don't know my name, so what's your game? I believe your name is Sol and you're out for a rag doll, latch on, Daddy, latch on? Your gims have the stare of the simple-brained square, trying to make a kill; Now if you need a thrill, your name must be Bill and the color of your paper must be green.

"I don't go for the bean, dear Mister Bill Green, I like my chops lean; and for a measure of pleasure and some sincere good cheer, put an egg and a half in my beer, that is if you're peddling nicotine. So, trilly, Mister Willie, you sound so silly, and besides, my Ace approaches; so make for your hole, Daddy-O, and save your roll if you don't go for them funeral coaches."

Was Red Riding Hood that Good?

(REQUIRES COUNTDOWN TO SET BEAT)

THIS LITTLE HI FI PIE wore some fire engine-hued threads from her cherry red head to her deuce of treads. The child was like wild and knew cats like Sweet Daddy Ed who played the chippies for his bread. Her wild oats she gave like to the goats— those with goat-ees; and she asked no fees neither copped any pleas. She craved to stink—in fresh ranch mink on a stool in a bar with some fat cat (a little ol' duke, or even Farouk) with a Continental car. That was her preference, though she was short on reference.

SHE FELT LIKE A DROOP AS SHE sat on her stoop and bemoaned her lack just as her Maw Squaw laid this shot on the rack: "Honeychile," she gummed as the Hi Fi hummed, "I got a basket that'll blow Ol' Granny's gasket. It's loaded with meat and lots of things sweet. There's an apple and a mess of scrapple. I put in some eggs and fried frog legs; some jello real mellow and a brief bit of beef as a spell of relief. There's cake and a milk shake, like soda pop and a scallop; a drip of suds for her thirsty old buds; some wine from a dandelion vine. I want you to beat out a light trot to Granny's pad—and don't you dare to speak to nary a lad while hitting the track to the Old Lady's shack."

"I WIG YOU AND DIG YOU," spieled the Hi Fi with a gleam in her eye. She'd never been out

FLEE

193

alone without her chaperon. At dances what few advances she got from the glad lads in the mad plaids had been intercepted by her old lady who shunned everything shady and wanted her daughter to act like she'd taught her—a perfect Joan of Arc out, man, to make her mark. So down the main stem, the Hi Fi with the glint in her eye knocked her stroll, her classy chassis all a-roll. She was thinking and shrinking, hoping, thinking of eloping with some broth of a lad with a real crazy Cad and a penthouse pad.

SUCH A LAD, HOWEVER, WAS ONE classified BAD. He had long pointed receivers and gims that were deceivers back of the smoked rimmers he wore on his glimmers. Like he was out for a nibble and would certainly not quibble, if it was togged in red from the treads to the head, especially one wild as was this child out singing "A-Tisket, A-Tasket," swinging her Granny's basket.

"HEY, HI FI," HE SOUNDED as his treads he grounded, "you're a real crazy little daisy. I'd like to pluck you—tuck you into my arm and shield you from harm; from the wolves and any dastard who claims to be plastered. Like if I wasn't so lazy, I'd take more time to praise thee. What you got that's both cool and hot—in that flasket, er-er, I mean basket?". . . "I've got some fine wine from the vine; something with a collar guaranteed to make you holler. I've got bird legs and hard-boiled eggs; French fried potatoes and softboiled tomatoes," spieled the Hi Fi with a gleam still in her eye. She had really dug this cat, man, from the tilt of his natural hat to the sound of his chat. And she was hip to his shape and the cut of his drape. She'd dug his chain and his famished Big Dane.

"MY MAW SQUAW cracked the whip and I'm copping the trip to visit Old Fanny, you see, she's my Granny. Like she's not doing so good in her pad in yon wood.". . . "Well," spieled the chap as his ears pierced his cap, "I'd like to help and if you need me, yelp. I'm in a hurry and must make my flurry as I weave a loom and knock a fast broom." Having thus spieled, he cut across the field and disappeared so fast, man, it was really quite weird.

AT GRANNY FANNY'S PAD, THE CAT WITH BIG EARS eased her queer fears as he jived through the slammer like a sidewalk flim-flammer. It was real cool, McPoole, the way the fool ate her up and left the bones for his beloved pup and nary a cone for Henry Jones. He put on her headpiece and then donned her fleece, looking like a clown in her flimsy nod gown. He jumped in bed and covered his head as the rap sounded on the outer flap.

THE HI FI WITH THE IDEA IN HER EYE, man, rushed to the nodder with the basket of fodder and copped her squat at exactly that spot and breathed a deep sigh that was not at all shy, for this broad had been pawed before by studs both rich and poor and was hep to the rep of this cat in Granny's flat. Since she dug him as the host, she was also hip that he was the most and she proposed this toast:

"Oh, Granny-O, what big gims you got!"... "Only to wig me to what is what and what is not," he shrilled ... "And Granny-O, what whale sized receivers—Jeeze! How they point!"... "Only that I might latch on to the sounds in this joint!"..."And what crumb-crushers you flash!"... "Only to help me render you into cool hash!"

THE CAT POPPED FROM THE LILYWHITES, like draped only in his sequined tights and the Hi Fi (the gleam gone from her eye) took off in a circle and like Fred Merkle (The '08 World Series donor—you remember, of course, his historic blunder?). She whaled straight for home—I hear 'twas to get her comb. She did, man, just like that Phfft! She was gawn! Well, the cat began drinking, probably thinking he'd missed his dinner and the Hi Fi was the winner, leaving him that much thinner. Figuring it now didn't matter, he put on a

platter—a bopper's chatter—and sat back to diddle with this
brand new riddle: *Just how he got stuck trying to pluck this delectable
duck.* Characteristically he said: *"It was just my bad luck!"*
JUST ABOUT THEN AS HE REACHED FOR THE GIN,
he looked around as he dug a new sound. He saw the Hi Fi,
now three quarters high, making her slow advance, her steady
glance demanding romance. Like her robes of red matched the
cherry of her head. That chick was on, man, I mean real gawn!
"Quit faking," she said as her robe (she invokes the 5th Amend-
ment here) she shed, "and tell me what's baking? Like I dig you
as a Wolf, Dad, a Wolf big and bad, who beat my Granny for
her pad. I decided to return from my homeward jaunt. Now
please hip me, Wolf, JUST WHAT DO YOU WANT?"
"A DINNER THAT'S THE MOST—I PREFER ROAST;
but since you ask, like it's no big task if it comes plain. You
know—some left over for my Big Dane . . ." "Well, what's on
the rail for this sweet little quail?" she said with a smile that
was devoid of guile. "And what's on the docket I can put in
my pocket? I have one love that's very distinct; it's my yen to
wear the most expensive in mink." . . . "Don't you worry about
any little thing," said the Wolf as he gnawed on a cold chicken
wing. "You're just a crazy, mixed up kid, but I'll hep you to
how the others did.
"SUE—SHE WAS PRETTY, A REAL COOL FOOL. Like I
put her through my finishing school. And there was the upsetting Della—she tells everybody I'm a most wonderful fella.
Now for you, I'll get you started on a diet of cash; enough for
a down payment on a '49 Nash. That should give me time to
think whether you're worth a short-tailed mink. But I'm a mite
careful with my fun and I never, never buy a pig in a bun!"
FROM THE WINE THE WOLF SHIFTED TO FOAM as
the Hi Fi reviewed quickly what she'd done at home. Like her
flaps then picked up a bit of a noise and she was hip right away
it was one of the boys. The Wolf turned around and nearly

blew his cap, as he dug the six-footer, a brute of a chap. He wanted to whistle for his Giant Big Dane, but recalled he let the hound play in the lane. His sky reverberated with schemes of escape, he didn't want this cat to mess up his new drape.

"HE ATE UP GRANNY, SWEET DADDY ED," the Hi Fi with much venom said. "He tried to put his bite on me, but I was just as hip as he. I lamped his ears and hungry chops and that was when I faded, Pops. But hold up Dad, on the rumble; this stud's got bread, so don't let us fumble. Man," she said, "That's Sweet Daddy Ed, he needs some fruit to knock a suit. Like he's mean as you can plainly see and only needs the nod from me to introduce you to some fistic bop. So give me your loot; I'll tell him to stop. I'm the new Red Riding Hood who means no slick Wolf any good. So, Dad, this really is the end, for no more Grannies will you rend. Never bet on a rural chick—if they're like me, they'll prove too slick. You dig me, Daddy-O?"

The Cool Cinderella

(ROCK 'N' ROLL WITH BASS VIOLS)

THE MILD CHILD wailed a whine to match her brine. Then she began putting down the action for the Boss Broad's satisfaction—hypes like busting the bugs from out of the rugs and striving with some mad pearl diving and dunking togs and rolling logs. 'Twas the slave tip, Rip. This Little Deal was all set to squeal because of her nowhere vines and her B-Flat nines. And her pony looked like dried macaroni. The poor little chick had no wick in her glims and no bounce in her stem. Man, she was a forgotten boll of cotton, Dig McSwig?

Well, the Boss Broad had moved into the dommie to get her three-a-bright salami from the Mild Child's Daddy-O who was tagged to grab the tab for the patio and to put down each seven a trip to this heaven (for the Boss Broad and her Brood—all rude and naturally crude)—so each and every could knock some food. You dig?

And Man, this was the dim for the hop on the stem and the bop was sure to pop as the cats and chicks went for the mix and dug the sounds as the young squares clowned. That's why the Boss Broad was so strong for her brood and she loudly mewed:

"I'm putting in the licks for my own nest of chicks. I'm putting you on so you'll be real gone when you fall in the hall and pick up the call to have a ball. At this frantic antic, I want you to know, you've simply got to steal the show. The Cat up there who leads the band, he's cool and way out and worth twenty grand. I want you to remember just what I said—if you have to, play dead to cop his shed. He's got a lotta extra loot and if you play him right, he'll knock you a suit along with the fruit. He's got some Caddys, two, three or four, and if any of you land him he'll buy five more."

The Brood of Young Hens really had their sins, cut plenty of rugs and washed dozens of jugs. They jived and connived with some smart and cool kids, some of them hep and wearing New York lids. They gnawed leather with a bunch of cats, and together they copped and bopped a bit trying to unload some of their mother-wit.

On the split-back at this crazy shack, the Band Cat came down and went to bat. He spieled out loud to the overflow crowd—

"All you chicks and broads and queens (and right now I'm hitting on the cool young teens), I'm set to wed and give up some bread to the one at this romp who can put on this stomp."

He picked up a box and cracked the locks so all could dig that wild golden rig shining clear and plain from that tog of cellophane.

"You chicks with the barkers, no need trying for these slides all have markers. I'm looking for the one with a shoeick, a tiny replica of a '60 Buick. Lean, long and slender, an aristocratic sender. Pickup, McGupp?"

There wasn't a wren there without the sin of having big dogs like small chunks of logs. The Brood got in the mood to get real rude when the Band Cat hollered "scat" and mugged to the oldest who was also the boldest:

"Hey you, blister, ain't you got a prettier sister?"

While all this jive was going down, at the Boss Broad's pad in a beat-up gown, the Mild Child finally smiled because a Chick on a Broom had zoomed into the room and with a delicate honk had stroked her conk with a long, slender stick that made the Mild Child a brand new chick. She came up with a crazy cape and an out there drape. After a short think, she weeded the Child a mink. At the curb, Herb, a chauffeured Caddy purred. The Mild Child fell in and with a happy grin, went off to the hall to have herself a ball. She lifted a raft of caps when she parted the flaps and broke on the scene, a real cool teen.

The Band Cat, still at bat, dug her from afar the moment she copped her stop in the bar.

"Send her down front," he said with a grunt. "Let her give this gold slide a ride."

Well, the Mild Child smiled again and it was like sunshine wailing through the rain. Her tiny treads fit the barkers just like a glove; didn't need the slightest shove.

"Stop the Music," the Band Cat howled while the disappointed chicks screamed and yowled. "This is a Mild Child and her name is Cinderella. I'm hipping everybody that I'm her fella. She's got a stomp like a miniature Buick, a real crazy trod, just dig that shoeick! From now on until I'm dead, she'll share my shed and spend my bread. The rest of you broads can sit in the bleacher while I drill with this chick to see the preacher."

Dig it? Man?

HIP SHEET...

HERE'S THE DEAL ON THIS CRAZY SPIEL—Mild Child—a gal real nice, you look at her twice. The action is work you can't shirk when the Boss Broad (stepmother named Maude) puts you to propositions (hypes) in the wrong position like shaking rugs and cleaning plates, silver and jugs which would be diving for pearls (in the sink, little girl). Dunk togs, oh ye dogs! That's washing clothes, Mose. Nowhere vines? Means clothes so worn the material shines and B-Flat nines are shoes in twos. Pony must have a tail and like dried macaroni, hers was frail. Wick in the glims means spark in the eyes and no bounce in the stems even (why should I be so wise?). Dommie is home whether in Tulsa or Rome and three-a-bright means thrice for the rice per day, Edna Mae. Tab for the patio means the rent for the tent and even seven is a week to drop in for a peek. The dim for the hop on the stem is the night for the dance at the Gem (ballroom or jukejoint—get the point?). Mix, you hicks, that means dancing, some call it prancing. Shed is house or home with a door and a bed. "Had their sins" means the girls had fun and that's no pun and washing jugs means drinking drinks (I know what you think!). To gnaw leather is to gobble steak while on the make. Split-black is midnight which is all right for the sight at the crazy shack—a joint from way back. Bread means money honey and a romp is a party so drink real hearty because a stomp means a shoe to those true blue. This one was gold, pretty and bold. Barkers are also shoes and good ones demand a lot of dues. A slide (another term for shoe) is good for a ride in a shoeick, which rhyming with Buick, is a shoe, too, Sue. A wren is a hen out on a bender and, naturally, of female gender. The Chick on the Broom was the fairy godmother and not the Mild Child's brother and conk is head, living or dead. Parting the flaps means entering the door (all good jive-bop lore). So, from here on out I hope you'll dig what the rest is about. It's a good deal, Della, this spiel about Cinderella. Chew some gum chum and admit it's crazy, huh, Daisy?

The Gawn Fawn

(REQUIRES FOUR BEERS, ONE HI-FI, ONE BROAD)

I was trigging my wig the other yawn and almost had a cloud-burst trying to beat out the stone that what young chicks don't dig about the red ticker would fill a knowledge mill of hip sheets. You latch on to these banters on the speed kick, cutting in and out of the stashes where the gone studs chew their cuds and crack the whips while the vet jets cop the trips, and when the young chicks wind up, they're still cutting in and out, still short of the green beat out on that machine.

She was a gone fawn, or at least she believed like what the cooties told her, and she figured she was due a promotion that would at least match her notion. So she put down the loud coca-cola crowd and started hunting bids from the fishtail boys with all that poise who make a lot of noise about their toys. Well, I dug the gone fawn as a filly named Lily and the fishtail stud as Cool Daddy Ed who was hip to all the ways of getting ahead. Now Cool Daddy Ed played it close to the chest and all he didn't palm he slipped in his vest. Like he was noted for his broads and for his numerous frauds since he was famed and blamed for kicking the gong and teaching little chicks how to do wrong.

And Cool Daddy Ed used to cop his bread cooling hides on occasional sides with Basie and Jess Stacy, Earl and Pearl and once in a while, a juke with the Duke. But his gimmin' of various women upset his red ticker and a slick chick gave him a nuzzle and in return he got her muzzle. Like, this was cool because he wanted it that way; you see, Cool Daddy Ed had to play dead while his books were in the red and that is where his chick (we'll call her Ella Slick) popped in port to take over his court.

She put him on some time when he didn't have a dime, and knocked him to some sous so he could really pay them dues!

Then she spieled, "No, my cool Daddy, I'm putting you in a Caddy and in some vines with the proper lines. When you cop your nod it won't be on the hard, cold sod. Like I'm stashing you between some lilywhites when old Hawk prowls on these chilly nights. I'm putting some hefty swag into your side bag, but don't (please tell me you won't) weed any to a hag when you're coasting in a Jag. I want my blood stud to be real great—plenty of green so he can rate. When it comes to a deal for a date, remember Gate, that I'm your mate!"

But Cool Daddy Ed, after he was properly fed, began making those plays for those crazy strays—chippies and chicks and banters and broads, Minnies and Connies and Sarahs and Maudes. He took from all and never gave—Cool Daddy Ed was a rugged knave.

While Ella Slick was on the pick, Cool Daddy Ed was getting ahead. The black he dug her like with another mug, the gawn fawn filly, we know as Lily, Ed was playing and parlaying, his gimmers straying and his roll displaying. The pad was leaping with a lot of creeping. Some were dancing, others were prancing. And some were drinking and like some were stinking as others, thinking, tried some winking without the blinking.

Then out of the smog—it was really a fog—all crazy and frantic and down-right romantic, the gawn fawn filly better known as Lily came through the slammer without using the hammer.

"I'm strictly for the vaunce in these familiar haunts! I'm looking for a stud with some love in his blood," she chattered as other broads scattered. "I know I'm young and on the last rung, but don't get me wrong, I really belong. All I need is a saddled steed. You can dig me but please don't wig me. I'm really on, this dawn!"

Cool Daddy Ed, trying to get ahead, dug her and latched and her line he matched.

"Come here, you mild child," she smiled. "Look, I'm well

fed. That's why I'm known as Cool Daddy Ed. The hip broads play dead like when they drop by my shed. I run my schools for Perfect Rums and fools and they call me Fess cause I weed 'em progress.

"I teach 'em how to reach, how to gab and how to grab, how to cut and how to butt. Some take lessons in conniving, others are happy with simple jiving. I teach 'em to get and not to give, so Cool Daddy Ed, himself, can live. Over me my broads often duel; like I beat and mistreat 'em because I'm just cruel. My fishtail burns up plenty of gas and the chicks that ride with me must have class. I'll flail a whale to make a sale. You're cute and you're young and I'll bet you ain't been hung. I'm the master with mustard plaster. Your first lesson is to obey, only me and not some stray. You got your learning because of your yearning for those cooties and cousin zooties, every one a tootie fruiti! I want you to know, this is the big show. I cool it and rule it, cause I'm Cool Daddy Ed, trying to make some more of that bread!"

Just about then he weeded her a fin and at the same time as the Ben hit the chime, through the slammer and spieling some bad grammar, drilled Cool Ed's Main Chick (we call her Ella Slick).

"Well, what do you know Joe?" she hissed real slow. "When I turn my back you snatch at a snack. Listen, boot, that's my loot and so is that suit and the sky you wear so high. So is the Caddy, my backbiting Daddy. Let's talk some shop before I chop. Like I gave you a pilt and a crazy quilt; bought you some shoes and I paid your dues. I gave you a horn to honk and cash to play tonk. I must have been on the red ticker kick. Now I'm no poet and you and I know it. But I'm a Jane from Spokane with a Lane from Fort Wayne. Now, Cool Daddy Ed, I don't want to whip your head. But I'll be a she panther like on this little banter if she don't disappear before I say beer. Now you've got the key, so come with me. She's a teen, but I'm the queen. So remember like you're ahead, but still my Cool Daddy Ed. Shall we broom from this room for our shed instead?"

–A–

Abie—The tailor

Ace—One, solitary, dollar, top-effort

Ace-deuce—Three, a trey

Ace-lane—Husband

Action—Motivating force, issue, situation, proposition

Action on a solid half traction—Ready to act, talk, commit an act

Air-bags—The lungs

Ain't coming on that tab (Abbr., "I ain't coming")—Refusal to coincide with a plan, an idea, etc.

Alligator-bait—A colored man, usually one from Florida

Alligator—Jitterbug

Anxious—Wonderful, excellent

Apollo play—Putting on an act

Apple—The earth, the universe, this planet. Any place that's large. A big Northern city where lines of color are not so pronounced as down yonder

Apron—A bartender, bar-keeper

Armstrongs—High trumpet notes

Asked his laces about the weather—Turned up toes

Attic—The head

Avenue-tank—A Fifth Avenue bus, double-decker bus

–B–

Baby kisser—Politician

Backbeat—Before, heart movement

Backbeat of the trey 30—Third day of the month

Backcap—A reply, a supplementary remark, a conclusion

Back gate parole—Death in prison

Bagpipe—Vacuum cleaner

Balloon room—Where marijuana is smoked

Ballroom without a parachute—Reefer den without reefers

Banana—Yellow girl, Mulatto, young, pretty

Bank—Toilet

Bantam—A young girl, a slender young woman, a sweetheart

Banta issues—Pretty girls

Banter—Pretty girl, 16 or 18

Banter play built on a coke frame—Young woman with a seductive shape on the order of a Coca-Cola bottle

Barbecue—A very attractive girl

Bark—Skin

Barkers—Shoes

Barrel house—Free and easy, low-down music, lowdown performance, in the vernacular

Basket—The stomach

Bats—Creaking old cronies chasing young men

Battle—A very unattractive girl

Beam—Get the range, see what one wants

Bean—Sun

Beat—Tired, not interesting, boring, ugly

Beater—Funds

Beat for the yolk—Without, or short of gold; money

Beat it out—Emphasize the rhythm, talk

Beat my own skin—Applaud

Beat the rocks—Walk the street

Beat up—Exhausted, unpleasant, tired, ugly

Beat up the chops—To converse freely

Beef—To talk loudly, to argue

Before Abe Jive—Slave, work (before Abraham Lincoln acted)

Beige—Tan, brown, light-colored Negro

Bender—Arm

Benders—The knees, the elbows, the arms

Benjamin or Benny—An overcoat

Bible—The absolute truth, a true statement, a true fact

Biddie—A cute little girl

Big Apple—Harlem, New York City, any Big Town

Big Red with the Long Green Stem—New York

City on Seventh Avenue
Big Wind (or Windy)—Chicago, the Windy City
Birdwood—Something to smoke, reefers
Biscuit—A pillow, the head
Black—Night
Black and Tan—Light and dark complexioned Negroes
Blew their tops—Went mad with excitement, with enthusiasm, gone crazy
Blindfolded lady with the scales—Justice; Court
Blinkers—Eyes
Blip—Very good, a nickel, five cents
Blow—To leave, move, run away
Blower—Handkerchief
Blow your top—Overcome with excitement, with pleasure
Blue—Sky, heavens
Blue Broadway—Heaven, Milky Way, way to Heaven
Bluff cuffs with the solid sender—Trousers with size 13 cuffs and ballooning
Bondage—In debt
Bonfire—Cigarette, or cigarette stub
Boogie-woogie—Eight to the bar harmony with accented bass achieved by playing fifths and thirds with the left hand; barrelhouse; manner of life

Boom-boom—Gun, cannon, rifle, shotgun, pistol
Boot—To tell, explain, understand, to comprehend, to perceive, describe, inform authoritatively
Booted me—Introduced me
Boot-snitch—Information, lexicon, a dictionary
Boulevard-cowboy—Taxicab driver
Boulevard-westerner—Wild taxicab driving, in manner of Chicago jitney cabs
Bouncy in one's deuce of benders—Scrape and bow in Uncle Tom fashion
Bow wow—Gun
Box—Piano, house, apartment, room
Box fire—Cigarette, or cigar stub
(The) Boys—Hustler, gang, the fellows on the corner, those who live the life
Brace o' broads—The Shoulders
Brace of hookers—Arms
Brace of horned corns—Aching feet with corns
Break it up—To score heavily
Bright—Day
Brightening—Early in the morning
Bring down—Not up to par, depressing, unseemly, out of place, wrong, not competent

Broad—Shoulder
Broom (noun)—Cigar
Broom (verb)—To walk,
run, flee, to move hur-
riedly away
Broom to the slammer that
fronts the drape crib—
Walk to the door of the
closet where your clothes
are kept
Brought—Downcast
Brown Abes and Buffalo
heads—Pennies and nickels
Brownie arcade—Penny
shooting and amusement
gallery
Brownie—Cent
Brush—The mustache,
to whip, to beat up, to
defeat, to conquer, to
skirmish with. "The
brush-off," etc.
Bugle—The nose
Bull—A Lesbian, a woman
with masculine inclina-
tions toward other
women
Bull's wool—Stolen clothes,
purloined goods
Bunch of fives—The fists
Bust your conk—Think hard,
work hard, go crazy
Butterflies—Pretty young
girls and women

–C–

Call off all bets—To die
Canary—Female singer,
yellow girl

Cap—To supplement, a
rejoinder
Capped—excelled, replied
Capon—Fairy, an effeminate
man (old or young)
Castle—A house, home,
room, apartment
Cat—The male of the
species, a boy, youth, or
man, one who knows
his way around; one
capable of taking care of
himself in any emergency;
one versed in worldly
knowledge, Jiver, a swing
musician
Cats not in—Those out of
US uniforms
Cat on the peek port—Look-
out man
Cat that cracks the whip—
Playboy, sportsman
Cats who long ago trilled—
Those who are dead
Cattle-train—A Cadillac car
Cave—A room, house, place
of abode
Chamber of Commerce—
Toilet
Charge—Marijuana cigarette
Chewers—The teeth
Chib or chiv—A switch-
bladed knife, a cutting
weapon of any sort
Chick—A young girl or
young woman. The Head-
Chick is one's sweetheart
or wife
Chicks that play hard
—Glamour girls; prosti-

tutes; good time girls
Chime—The hour
Chimer—An alarm clock, watch, or time-piece of any sort, the heart
Chimer-bell—A bell, a clock, watch, one's heart
Chimney—A top-hat, the head
Chippie—Glamour girl, play girl, slender, young girl of the racy, bony type
Chirp—Young girl vocalist, bird
Choker—Tie
Cholly—A dollar bill
Chops—The lips, the mouth, the legs, the hips
Chinchpad—A hotel, a cheap rooming-house
Clambake—A swing session, every man playing at random
Claws—Fingers
Clip—To deprive one of something, to steal, to cheat, to clip like a shorn lamb
Clip side of big moist— Other side of ocean where shooting is going on
Clipped—To have one's bankroll taken
Clink—Colored man
Clock or clocker—The heart
Cluck—Black, very dark
Coffee-bag—A pocket
Coke-frame—A body stream-lined like a Coca-Cola bottle

Cold meat party—A funeral
Collar—To take hold of, grab, understand, comprehend
Collar a broom—To leave
Collar a duster up the ladder—Climb the steps
Colts—Young men, boys
Come again—Repeat what you're saying, I don't understand you
Comes on like Gang Busters—Doing something in a terrific way
Come to school—To "give in," to acquiesce, learn
Conk—The head, hair, grease for the hair, pomade, brain, thinking faculties
Conkpiece—The head
Copper-nose—A drunkard
Cop—Take, understand, walk, conceive, consider, appeal to, work
Cop a broom—To leave hurriedly
Cop a drill—Leave quickly, disappear, or walk away, saunter, stroll, meander, pass away, succumb, die
Cop a squat—To be seated, to sit down
Corn—Money
Corny—Out of date, old, trite
Cow express—Shoe leather
Cracked-ice—Diamonds
Creaker—An aged person
Crib—House, apartment, room, home, bed

Crumb crunchers—The teeth, molars

Crumb-hall—Dining room

Crumb-stash—Dining room, kitchen

Cruncher—The street, sidewalk, road

Cute suit with the loop droop—Suit whose coat is similar in length to a frock or cutaway jacket

Cut out—To disappear, to leave

Cut rate—To belittle a person, play cheaply

Cutware bottoms up—Glass turned up in process of drinking

—D—

Dagger-pointed goldies—Sharp-toed yellow shoes

Davy Crocketts—Trappers, draft board officials

Daddy week—Frank Schiffman, managing director, Harlem's famous Apollo Theatre (week refers to length of employment by Mr. Schiffman to acts and bands)

Dead President—A dollar bill, paper money of any denomination

Deece—A dime

Defense plant on square's dim—Harlem's Apollo Theatre Amateur Night

Deep six—A grave

Deep sugar—A sweet line of talk, light banter

Demon—Dime

Den—House, apartment, room, home

Desk piano—Typewriter

Deuce—Two, a pair, a dime, ten cents

Deuce o' dims and darks on the cutback—Two nights and days ago

Deuce of benders—Knees

Deuce of demons—Two dimes, twenty cents

Deuce of haircuts—Two weeks

Deuce of nods on the backbeat—Two nights before

Deuce of peekers—Eyes

Deuce of ruffs (russ)—Twenty cents

Deuce of squares—Two rather average fellows with an overbalanced belief in their ability to move about in fast company

Deuce of ticks—Two minutes

Dicty—Snobbish, upper class

Dig—To understand, consider, appeal to, to comprehend, to remember, to sample, take, conceive, perceive, think, hand over

Dig the dip on the four and

two—Take a bath on Saturday; bathe every six days
Digs the dipper for some brine—Ask the bartender for a beer
Dim—Evening, night
Dime note—Ten dollar bill
Dims and brights—Days and nights
Dims and brights unhipped on the black and whites—Days ahead seem dark and dreary both night and day
Dip—Hat
Doghouse—Bass fiddle
Dome—The head
Dommie—House
Doss—Sleep
Down with it—To understand, know, to be ready for action
Drag—Disappoint, sorrowful, humiliate, upset, disillusion, a bore, uninteresting, bothersome
Drape—suit of clothes, outer garments
Dreambox—The head
Dreamers—Bed covering
Dribble—Stutter
Dried-barkers—Furs
Drilling—Walking
Drink—Ocean, river, sea, water, stream
Drumsticks—Legs
Dry goods—Outer garments, clothing
Dry long so—That's the way it goes, fate, manner of acting or talking, droll

Ducks—Tickets
Duds—Clothes
Dukes—Knees, fists
Dust—To leave
Dust-bin—A grave

—E—

Early beam—In the morning
Early black—In the evening
Early bright—Morning
Eighty-eight (88)—Piano
Enamel—Skin
Evil—In a bad mood
Expense—Newborn baby

—F—

Face—A white person
Fall out—To be aroused emotionally, to be taken by complete surprise
Feelers—Fingers
Fell—To be put in prison, or durance vile
Fews and twos—Small quantity of money
Few tickers—A few minutes
Fiddle-cases—Shoes
Fillmill—Tavern
Filly—Young girl, or woman
Final—To leave, to go
Finale—Death, last out
Final trill—Death
Fine—All right, okay, excellent
Fine banana—A pretty, yellow colored girl
Fine dinner—An attractive female

Fine fur—Fur coat
Fine fryers—Pretty young girls, chicks
Fire—Cigarette
First 30—January
Fish-hooks—Fingers
Fish horn—Saxophone
Fives—Fingers
Fizzical culturist—Bartender
Flag spot—Bus stop
Flappers—Arms
Flaps—Ears
Flat—Nickel, five cents, apartment, broke
Flickers—Moving pictures
Flippers—Ears
Flychick—Young girl about 18 or 20 years old, a pretty girl, a gay young lass, a girl who makes pleasure the foremost consideration in her life, a girl who knows all the answers
Flyer with the roof slightly higher—Hat similar to a modified ten gallon Stetson
Focus—To look, to see
Forks—Fingers
Four and one—Friday
Foxy—Clever, smart
Frail—The girl friend, a slender young girl or woman, poor, poverty-stricken
Frame—The body, skeleton, a suit of clothes
Frantic—Great, wonderful
Fraughty issue—A bad condition, a discouraging or sad message
Freeby—Free, without charge
Fresh water trout—Pretty girls
Frisking the whiskers—Musicians playing a few bars before a swing session
Frolic pad—Show, nightclub, theatre
Front—Wearing apparel
Fruiting—Playing around promiscuously
Fry—Process of having irons put on hair to remove kinks

–G–

Gabriel—Trumpeter
Gage—Marijuana cigarette, liquor, intoxicant
Gal officers—Harpies, Lesbians
Gam cases—Stockings
Gammin'—Boasting, showing off
Gams—Legs
Gaper—A mirror
Gas—Story, to talk, conversation
Gas buggy—Automobile
Gasper—A cigarette
Gas pipe—Trombone
Gassed the scribe—Thrilled girl by conversation
Gasser—Something that is tops, great, excellent, something that thrills or delights, an enjoyable

occurrence or situation, that which gives pleasure, a story packed with action, a car

Gate—A male

Gatemouth—One who knows everyone else's business

Gator—Swing music fan

Gazer—Window

Get in there—To become active, to exert your best efforts

Gims—The eyes

Gimme some skin—Slap hands in greeting

Gimming—Looking one over

Gimming every play—Sizing up soft touches

Gin mill—Bar

Glad pads—Fun spots

Glory roll—One's bank account, one's money

Go-down—A cellar or basement apartment, the basement or subterranean abode

Got your boots on—A hep cat

Goo—Food, dinner, sticky food, blood

Goo-goo watch—Early morning

Goola—Piano

Go-up—An upstairs apartment

Go-up Salt River—Die

Grabbers—Hands (arms, fingers)

Grape-cat—Male devotee to wine

Grape-chick—Female devotee to wine

Grass—Short hair

Grass-reefers—Marijuana cigarette

Gravy—Gains in relation to money

Grease—To eat

Great White father—President of the United States

Green banana—Young yellow girl, young mulatto

Grey—A white person, Nordic

Grey issue on the cornpone side of the black and white split—Situation with the white folks down South across Mason-Dixon Line

Grey who wouldn't play the game like it should be played—White person who doesn't act right

Groan box—Bass fiddle

Groovy—In keeping with a situation, the best thereof, highly enjoyable and/ or entertaining, superb, great, tops, excellent

Ground apple—Stone, brick, rock

Groundgrabbers—Shoes, feet

Groundpad bag—Socks

Groundpads—The feet, shoes

Groundpad Spade—Shoe horn

Growl—Trumpet notes

Gums—The lips, the mouth
Gutbucket—A low place, or
music
Gun—Look over

—H—

Half a stretch away—Half a
block
Half past a colored
man—12:30 AM
Hams—Legs, hips
Hard—Fine, excellent
Hard-hitting—Class, up-to-
date, nice-looking
Hard Johns—FBI agents
Hard-Oil—Butter, oleomar-
garine, lard
Hard skull fry—Heavy, shiny
conk hair-do
Hard spiel—Jive talk
Harlem-toothpick—Pocket-
knife, switchblade, knife
Harpies—Old, designing
women
Hatchet-thrower—Spaniard,
Cuban, Latin American
Having a ball—Having a
good time
Hawkins—Cold winter wind
Hawk riding—Refers to
Coleman Hawkins,
famous saxophonist,
playing his popular "Body
& Soul" on a phonograph
record
Head-chick—The wife or
sweetheart
Head hen—Landlady
Head Knock—The Lawd

Headlights—Diamonds
Heavy heat stretch—
Summer
Heavy lard—A story to be
told
Heavy lump—Sugar Hill
Heavy wet—Rain
Hemp—Marijuana cigarette
Hen—Any woman over 29
Hen tracking—Signing your
name
Hep—To be aware of, to
have attained a degree of
understanding, the ability
to perceive quickly, to
know, to be competent,
the business of being alert
Hep cat—A male who knows
all the answers
Herd—A pack of Camel
cigarettes
Hideaways—Pockets
Hidebeater—A drummer
Hides—Smooth skin, drums
High hard yard—Hard stiff
collar
High-powered—Up-to-date,
nice looking
Hike—Lay away, treasure,
put aside
Hincty—Snobbish, aloof,
conceited
Hinges—Elbows
Hinges creaking—Getting
old, aging, senility
Hip—See "hep"
Hip chick—Girl, counterpart
of cat
Hipped Spade—A Negro
who knows the score

Hocks—Feet
Home-cooking—Something
fine
Homey—One newly arrived
from the south, a person
from one's hometown,
one who isn't fully aware
of what is going on
Honkin' Brown—A loud
colored suit
Hooks—Fingers
Hoop—A ring
Hop—To cavort, to dance,
to jump, to leap, to play
Hop a twig—Die
Hot—Expression used
before "swing" music to
express degree of perfec-
tion of jazz music
Hotbed—A bed used by
three or four persons
sleeping in relays in eight
hour shifts, for the price
of 25 cents
House of countless drops—
Bar and grill
House without chairs where
the lights are a solid
blue—Good time flat,
ballroom, shady rendez-
vous
Hummer—Free, getting by,
getting something for
which nothing is paid,
exceptionally good
Hush hush—A pistol,
revolver
Husk—Undress
Huskings—What is left
Hustle—Beg, not work,

to borrow, to live by
one's wits or ingenuity,
request. A way of life as a
prostitute, playboy, pimp,
or tramp. Unconventional
action of some sort
Hustler—A beggar, one who
refuses to work, a playboy,
prostitute, lady of leisure,
tramp, an illegitimate
performer
Hype—A plot, a trick, a
scheme or design to take
advantage of someone, or
of a situation, a proposition, usually phoney. An
idea of swindling some-
one. The act of begging
for something. To think
up a scheme with the
intent of tricking or taking
advantage of someone

–9–

Ice-palace—Jewelry store
Icky—Conservative musi-
cian
Idea pot—Head
Igg—To refuse to notice,
disregard willfully, to
ignore
In and outer—Door
Index—Face
Insider—Pocket
In there—A superb situa-
tion, a thrill, a top-flight
performance, truly great,
wonderful. If applied
in a sartorial sense, it

means well-dressed,
really tops
In the groove—Excellent,
okay, all right, perfect
Israelite—A Jew
Issue—Situation, case,
thing, person, people,
intangibles

—J—

Joint is jumping—Place is
lively with entertainment,
with fun, etc.
Jolly boy—A kite
Joy-hemp—Reefer, mari-
juana cigarette
Joy roots—Reefers, mari-
juana cigarettes
Jug—A drink, a bottle, jail
Juice—Liquor
Jump—Frolic, have fun,
dance, swing-music,
pleasure, to leap in time to
music
Jumped in port—Came to
town unexpectedly
Jack—Refers to a male
Jackson—A form of address
used in speaking to a
colored man with whom
one is familiar
Jam—Spontaneous swing
music
Jeff—Someone who is not
interesting, a pest
Jelly—Without charge
Jersey side of snatch play—
Over 38 years old
Jesse James Killer—Heavy,

glue-like hair grease
Jin—Indian
Jitter bug—One who is a
swing music addict
Jitterdoll—Female dance
lover
Jitter Jane—Female dance
enthusiast
Jive—A style of talking and
writing, Harlem slang, a
commodity, anything that
is tangible, that which is
intangible and pertains
to a manner of living and
thinking, hot music, hot
dancing, fooling someone,
flattery, to sneer at, to be
cynical of, to cajole
Jiver—A hepcat, a Harlem
sophisticate, who knows
what it is all about, a person
"hepped," who knows
exactly what to do or say
under any circumstances
Joe blow—Musician, any
male
John—A square, jaded, white
male seeking thrills in
colored communities

—K—

Kemels—Shoes
Keyholing a round tripper—
Looking at something
really beautiful, i.e.,
round-tripper—a home
run
Kick—A pocket
Kicks—Thrill, ecstasy, shoes,

the feet, enthusiasm
Kill—To thrill, fascinate,
enthrall
Kill joy—Policeman
Kill me—Entertain me, show
me a good time
Killer-diller—Great, won-
derful, a thrill
Kiss-off—Death
Kite—Air mail letter
Kite with no string—Air
mail and first class letters
Knobs—Knees
Knock—To put down, speak,
walk, loan, borrow, give,
ask, exhibit
Knock a nod—To go to
sleep, the act of sleeping
Knocking her dead one on
the nose each and every
double trey—Getting paid
every six days
Knocking off hen tracks on
a roll top piano—Writing
letters on a typewriter
Knock off—To die
Knock play—Those who will
lend
Knotholes—Doughnuts
Knowledge-box—The brain,
the head
Kong—Whiskey, moonshine
liquor
Kopasetic—Excellent, tops,
okay

—£—

Laid down the cow—Laid
down shoe leather

Lamb—One who is easy
pickings for gamblers,
jivers, high pressure
salesmen, etc.
Lamp—Look, to see, to view
Lamps—Eyes
Land O'Darkness—Negro
settlement in any town,
Harlem
Land of many squints—
Orient
Lane—One who doesn't
understand, a hick, a smart
aleck, a confidence man
Larceny laid down on all
issues—Manner in which
a situation is discussed
Last debt—Death
Last out—Death
Latch—To understand, take,
perceive, think, meet
Latch for the gate to your
front yard—Collar pin
Latch on—Understand, to
take, to think
Late black—Late night
Lay—Put down, speak, walk,
hide, give, ask, exhibit
Laying your knowledge—
Taking advantage of a
situation
Layout—House, apartment,
room, store,
office, place, business
establishment
Layout across the drink—
Continent of Europe
Lay your racket—To kid, to
be shrewd
Lead sheet—Outer coat,

such as topcoat or over-
coat
Left raise—Left side
Leg sacks—Socks
Lemon—Yellow girl,
Mulatto, a man
Let him down for his
chimer—Stole his watch
Licking the chops—Musi-
cians tuning up before a
jam session
Licks—Hot musical note
Lid—Hat, headgear, cap, the
head, brain
Light drip-drizzle—Rain
Lightning bugs—Lighted
cigarettes in a darkened
room
Light splash—Bath
Like cheese—Odor
Lilywhites—Sheets, bed covers
Lip Splitter—Wind musician
Line—Purchase price or cost
in terms of money
Line the flue—To eat
Locked up—To have sole
possession of
Long ones with many
links—Key chain
Long white roll—Cigarette
Love letter—Missile, bullet,
a stone, a rock, thrown
with malicious intent
Lugs—Ears
Low-quarters—Shoes,
oxfords
Lung-duster—Cigarette
Lush—Drink, strong liquor,
whiskey, wine, beer
Lush head—Drunkard

Lushie—Drunkard
Lush-stash—Saloon, bar, grill

–M–

Mad—Fine, capable, able,
talented
Man who rides the scream-
ing gasser—Police patrol
Main drag—Seventh Avenue
Main drag of many tears—
126th Street where
disappointment tinges the
loud laughter
Main kick—The stage
Main on the hitch—Boy-
friend, husband
Main queen—Girl-friend,
wife
Main stem—Principal
avenue, main corner, a
street hangout
Main trill—Street
Man in gray—Postman
Man with the book of many
years—The judge, court,
jurist
Map—The face
Marble town—Cemetery
Mash me—Give me
Mason—Line dividing
America, North and
South
Mass action—Communism
Mellow—Fine, the tops,
excellent, superior, great,
superlative
Mellow-blacks—Pretty black
girls
Mellow drag and has the

sag—Same as cute suit
with loop droop
Mellow roof—Head
Melted out—Down and out,
without any money
Mess or messy—That which
one likes, a state of mental
or physical excitement,
pleasure
Meter—Twenty-five cents
Mezz—Tops, sincere
Midway—Hall, corridor,
hallway
Mighty Dome—House of
Congress, the Capitol, a
place where laws are made
and debates are held
Mikes—The ears
Mister Hawkins—The wind,
winter time, cold weather,
ice, snow
Mister Speaker—A gun,
revolver
Mitt pounding—Applause
Mooch—To beg, to borrow,
to sponge on another
Moo juice—Milk
Mop—Period, the end,
expressed action, final
method of doing
Mose—Negro
Moss—The hair
Mow the lawn—Comb the hair
Mouse—Pocket
Mug—The face, to grimace,
to make love, to rob
Mugged behind five—Talk-
ing behind palm of hand
Muggin'—Making faces,
making love

Murder—Tops, fine
Mush—Kiss

–N–

Napoleon—Insane man,
crazy
Neighbo Pops—That's out,
Chum, no chance
New double six—12 and a
new year
Nickel note—A five dollar
bill
Nickelette—Juke-box,
phonograph machine into
which nickels are put
Nix out—To discard, to get
out of
Nod—Rest, sleep
Noisola—Phonograph

–O–

Ofay—White person
Ofay sweet-smell—White
talcum powder, lilies
Office piano—Typewriter
Off the cob—Backward,
trite, outdated
Off time jive—Banter, sorry
excuse
Oil—To whip, to beat,
money
Oiled head—Whipped head
Oiler—One who will fight
Old saw—The wife, old girl
friend, a common-law
wife
Old man Mose—Father
Time, death

Onion act—Stinking
act, something wrong,
uncalled for
On the beam—Smart,
knowing, in the groove, in
mood for jiving
On the beam on short cut
plays—Smart as to what's
going on
Orchestration—An overcoat
Out of this world—Excel-
lent, tops
Oxford—Black, Negro

—P—

Pad—House, apartment,
room, home, bed
Paddles—The hands
Pail—The stomach
Paper doll—Playing hooky,
leaving, cutting out
Pan—The face
Panicky—Extreme pleasure,
excitement over some-
thing
Paws—The hands
Pay offs—Patrons
Pecking—A dance intro-
duced at Cotton Club in
1937
Peckings—Food
Peekers—the eyes
Peeps dig the range—Eyes
take in the scene
Peeling a fine green
banana—Making love to a
pretty yellow girl
Pegs—Trousers
Peola—An extremely light-
complexioned person
Phiz—The face
Piccolo—Juke-box, music
machine
Pickers—The fingers
Pick-up—Take action, do,
act, perceive, conceive,
understand, to gather
an impromptu meal
together
Pies—Eyes
Pigeon—A young female
Pigeon dropping—Playing
confidence games
Pile of bricks—A house, a
building
Pillars—The legs
Pimp steak—Frankfurter
Pinchers—Shoes
Pine drape—A coffin
Pink or pinktoe—White girl
Pins—The legs
Pistols—Zoot trousers
Play—Situation, issue, plan,
program, idea,
viewpoint, a girl
Playing the dozens with
one's uncle's
cousins—Doing every-
thing wrong
Plates—The feet
Platters—The Feet
Plunger—A bathtub
Poke—A purse, one's money,
funds
Poop out—To fail, to crack up
Pops—A greeting for all
males
Pops in port—To arrive, to
come on the scene

Poppa-stoppa—Any old man, a professor
Popper—Gun, pistol, revolver
Portrait—Face
Pounders—Detectives, policemen
Pour man—Bartender
Prayer bones—The knees
Prayer dukes—The knees
Prayer handles—The knees
Props—The legs
Puffed air—No food
Pulleys—Suspenders
Pumpkin—The moon, sun
Puss—The face
Put down—Say, perform, describe, do
Putting the issue on someone—Giving him a uniform, a gun, and the military training to go with it

–R–

Racket-jacket—Zoot suit
Rag—Magazine or newspaper
Rag out—To dress up
Rah-rah drapes—Collegiate-styled clothing
Rank—To degrade
Rat hole—Pocket
Ready—Looking just right, dressed nicely, feeling in the right mood for action
Reefer—Marijuana cigarette, dope, narcotic, a cigarette
Repent pad—A playboy's

apartment where a girl is lured to repent later
Riceman—Chinese
Ride—To keep perfect time
Riff—Musical licks
Riffs and rills—Propositions, ideas, plans
Righteous—Tops, the acme of perfection, fine, enjoyable, the quintessence of a situation or thing, superlative, incomparable, something unusually pleasing to the senses, pretty, lovely, something definitely out of the ordinary
Righteous cool—Nice day
Righteous riff—Engaging line of conversation
Righteous yellows—Pretty mulatto girls
Rind—The skin
Ripper—One who uses a knife, one who has a bad reputation
Roach—Marijuana cigarette, dope, narcotic
Rock—Supreme pleasure, tops in dancing and music, finest esthetic delight, a dollar
Rock candy—Diamonds
Rock me—Delight me, excite me, send me
Rockpile—Skyscraper building
Rommel—Did an about face, like the Nazi General
Roost—House

Rope—Marijuana cigarette
Rubber—Automobile
Rudolph Hess—Fade away
Ruff—Twenty-five cents
Rugcut—To dance, cavort,
gambol, enjoy dancing
without paying for the
privilege as at a house-
party, to play around
Rugcutter—One who dances
in an apartment, one who
would dance and not pay,
one who cuts the carpet with
his dancing but buys nothing

–S–

Sad—Distasteful, bad, not
enjoyable, pitiful
Sadder than a map—Very
bad, terrible, disgusting
Safety—Bed
Sails—The ears
Salty—Disagreeable, in a bad
mood, angry
Sam got you—Inducted into
the Army
Saw—Landlady
Scarf—Food, meal, dinner
Scoff—Food, dinner, a meal,
to eat, to dine
Scoffing fishheads and
scrambling for the gills—
Having a hard time of it
Scoffings—What you eat
Scratch-crib—Cheap hotel,
rooming house
Screaming-gasser—Patrol
wagon, police-squad car
Scuffle—To work for a
living at some legitimate
occupation, to dance
Scuffler—Workman, daily
laborer, one who earns his
living through legitimate
efforts
Send—Thrill, stir enthusi-
asm, exuberance, gratified
Set of seven brights—Seven
days, a week
Shafts—The legs
Sharp—Distinctive, smart,
outstanding
Shiv (or chib)—Pocket
knife, switchblade, dagger
Shoeick—The feet
Shooting the marbles from
all sides of the ring—To
be in a position to take
action
Short trills—Abbreviated
walks, within walking
distance
Shuck dropping—Taking
advantage of someone
Shutters—The eyes
Signifying—To say in a
double-meaning manner
Six—Grave
Skate—To get by without
paying, to dodge the tariff
Skiffling and skuffling—
Feverish activity
Skin-beater—Drummer
Skins—Drums
Sky—Hat, headgear, helmet
Sky-piece—Hat, headgear,
helmet
Sky-pocket—Inside vest or
coat pocket

Skull—One who is a top
performer, an ace slicker
Slab—Bread
Slammer—Door, portal,
entrance
Slanters—The eyes
Slap-happy—A swing-music
addict
Slave—To work
Slave tip—Work, job
Slicing their chops—Talking
Slide your jib—to talk
openly, to talk easily
Slides—Shoes
Slops and slugs—Coffee and
doughnuts
Smit Smoke—Smart Negro
Smoke screen—Deodorant
Snap a snapper—Light a
match
Snapper—Match
Snatcher—Policeman,
detective
Sneezer—Handkerchief
Sniff a powder—To go away,
to run out
Sniffer—The nose
Snip a dolly—To cut out, to
leave, to become absent
Snipe—Cigar or cigarette stub
Snitch-sheet—Newspaper,
magazine, pamphlet
Snitch-pad—Notebook
Snitcher—Newspaper
report, an informer, a
writer, a columnist
Snuffer—The nose
Sock frock—Best suit
So help me—That's the truth
Soft-top—Stool

Solid—Essence of perfec-
tion, absolute tops in the
way of performance, the
acme of any technique
great, truly wonderful,
exciting, excellent,
marvelous. A sensational
thrill of some sort
Solitaire—Suicide, to kill
oneself
Sounded off—Began conver-
sation
Sou—Nickel or coin
Spade—Negro
Splash—Water, bathe, ocean,
lake
Spark—Match, light, ciga-
rette, star, diamond
Spic—Spanish-American,
one of Latin extraction
Spiel—To talk, discuss,
or make a speech, to
describe, tell in detail,
give a complete account
of. A declaration, sup-
plication, or dissertation.
To orate, to converse
Spin a hen or Spin a wren—
To dance with a woman
Spinning at the track on
fool's dim—Dancing at
the ball room on a maid's
night out
Spook—A colored person, or
a white man
Spotters—The eyes
Spoutin'—Talking a great
deal, talking too much
Square—One who works
for a living, who is on the

square, an honest person,
one with money, one
who chases women and is
taken for his money
Squat—To sit down
Squatpad—A stool, a chair
or lounge
Squatter—A stool, a chair
Squeezer—Belt
Stache—To hide away, to file
Stand one up—To under-
rate a person, to play one
cheap
Stash—to hide, stand,
conceal, layaway, a
stool, a seat, place
Stashed—To stand or remain
Stashing—Remaining,
standstill
Stealers—The fingers
Stems—The legs
Step-off—The curb
Stewers—Old women
Stewie—A drunkard
Stick—A drunkard
Sticks—Marijuana cigarette
Stiffing the stroll—Standing
on the corner
Stilts—The legs
Stir—Jail
Stompers—Shoes
Stomps—Shoes
Stooling—Snitching, telling
on someone, giving away
the truth
Straps—Suspenders
Streamer issue—Necktie
Street—Road
Stretcher—The neck, a belt,
suspenders, straps

Striders—Trousers
Strides—Trousers
Striding—Playing ten key
stretches in bass on piano
Stroll—Road
Stroll street—Trail
Stud—A man, male
Stud-hoss—An appellation,
used by way of greeting,
a male
Stud with many fingers—J.
Edgar Hoover and his FBI
Stumble—To get into
trouble, misfortune, dire
predicament
Stumbled and fell—Got into
trouble and went to jail
Stumps—The legs
Suffering with the shorts—
Broke, down and out
Susie-Q—Dance introduced
at Cotton Club in 1936
Swobble—To eat hurriedly,
greedily
Swimps and wice—Shrimps
and rice, a way of saying that
one can get what he wants
Switch—Knife

—T—

Tab action—To borrow,
request a loan
Tab issue—Asking, begging,
borrowing
Tabs—Ears
Tagged the play with the
slammer issue—Solved
the problem by putting
the culprit in jail

Take a powder—Leave, disappear
Take it on—Eat
Take it slow—Be careful
Take off—Hips
Take off—Play a solo
Tattler—Alarm clock, watch
Tea—Marijuana cigarette, dope
Tears—Pearls
Ten—Toes
Ten bones—Fingers
That's what she wrote—Final, the end, period
The bank—Toilet
The man—The law
Thinkbox—Brain
Thinkpad—Head, brain
Thin one—A dime, ten cents
Threads—Clothes, a dress, garments
Three-pointer—Corner
Three-pointer of the ace trill in the twirling top—Corner on the main street; Seventh Avenue in Harlem
Tick—Minute
Ticker—Heart, watch
Tick-tock—Heart
Timber—Tooth picks
Tinkler—Bell, doorbell
To fall—To go to jail, to be imprisoned, punished
To gas—To thrill, to overcome, to stir the emotions
Togged to the bricks—Dressed completely in height of fashion
Too much—Used to express highest degree of praise
Tootin' stomps—Low-quarter shoes
Top-flat—Head
Topper—Hat
Top Sergeant—A Lesbian, a lady lover
Topside of rockpile—Sixth floor of an apartment building
Tower of Pisa—Leaning
Track—Dance hall, a ballroom
Trap—Draft board
Treaders—Shoes
Tree-suit—Coffin
Trey—Three
Trey of sous—Three nickels
Trey of sous and a double ruff—Forty cents
Trickeration—Strutting my stuff
Trigging my wig—Cudgeling my brain
Trig the wig—Think quickly
Trill—Walk, stroll in a mincing manner, strut
Trilling—Fancy stepping
Trilly—To walk, to come to, to go away from, to amble
Trilly-walk—To leave, move on foot, run, fly, strut
Trods—Feet
Trotters—Feet, legs
Truck—To move, to leave, to go
Trucking—A dance introduced at Cotton Club in 1933

Trumped the hump—
  Climbed the hill
Tube—Subway
Tune in our mikes—To
  listen
Turf—Sidewalk street
Turtles—Turns
Tweed boy—Scotchman in
  kilts
Twig—Tree
Twigs—Legs
Twinkle—Doorbell
Twinklers—The eyes
Twister—Key, means of
  entry
Twister to the slammer—
  Key to the door
Two Camels—Ten minutes,
  an interval of time
Two cents—Two dollars
Two-story lorries—Dou-
  bledecker buses

—U—

Uncle—Pawnshop operator
Uncle Sam's action—Induc-
  tion
Under the wire—To score
Unglamorous—Unsavory,
  cheap, shoddy, bad, ugly,
  wrong
Unhep—A Square, unaware
  of what's going on
Unhipped—One who
  doesn't know, state of
  being unaware of the true
  state of affairs or what is
  going on

Uprights—Legs
Upstairs—Heaven, the sky,
  the brain

—V—

Vacuum cleaner—Lungs
Vine—Clothing
V-8—An unfriendly female,
  female who doesn't want
  company

—W—

Waders—Boots
Walk-back—Rear apartment
Walk down—Basement
  apartment
Washer—Saloon, tavern,
  grill
Waters—Boots
Water works—Crying eyes
Wear a smile—To go nude
Weed—Give, hand, lend,
  pass over
Weed—Marijuana cigarette,
  dope, narcotic, a cigarette
Weed a holler note until his
  mudder came in—Loaned
  him a 100 bill until his
  horse came in
Weepers—Mourning gar-
  ments, funeral attire
What's your story?—How are
  things, what excuse do you
  have, what do you want
Wheel-chair—Automobile
Whipped up—Tired out,
  exhausted

White one—A shirt
Wig—Head, brain, mentality
Wigglers—Fingers
Windbag—Lungs
Wind pumps—Lungs
Windy City—Chicago
Wolf—A male who chases
women
Wolverine—A woman who
chases men
Wren—A girl
Wringling and twist-
ing—Discrimination and
segregation
Wrong riff—The wrong thing,
either by words or action

Yam—To eat
Yarddog—An uncouth male
or female

Yeah, man—An exclamation
to express something in
the affirmative
Yellow eye—An egg
Yoke—Jitterbug collar
Young bantam—Little girl

—Z—

Zoom—To get in free, to
obtain something for nothing, to get by when one is
penniless, slipping in where
admission is charged
Zoot suit—Clothes that are
extreme in style, overexag-
gerated
Zoot suit action—Zoot wars

Editor's Notes

1. The full citation for the article to which Conrad refers is Earl Conrad, "The Philology of Negro Dialect," *Journal of Negro Education* 13 (Spring 1944): 150–54.

2. Conrad here intends "Nize Baby." He refers to an illustrated column in the *New York World* by cartoonist and columnist Milt Gross, "Gross Exaggerations." As Conrad notes, the column parodied the stereotypical Jewish immigrant dialect by depicting mothers telling fairy tales to appease a "nize baby." In 1926, Gross published the columns in a book titled *Nize Baby*. See Milt Gross, *Nize Baby* (New York: George H. Doran, 1926).

3. Though the A. Wendell Malliet Company began publishing in 1942, Malliet is not listed in the catalog information in Burley's *Handbook*, which was self-published. Malliet also served as a foreign correspondent for the *New York Amsterdam News*. The connection to that paper is probably the source of the two's relationship.

4. In 1945, a year after the *Handbook*'s publication, John H. Johnson created a new magazine to accompany *Negro Digest, Ebony*, in Chicago. Six years later, in 1951, Burley would return to Chicago from New York to work for *Ebony* and the newly created *Jet*.

5. The "Jiver's Bible," a functional glossary of terms, originally appeared at the back of the *Handbook* but for the sake of convenience and continuity appears at the back of this volume, following the *Handbook*'s sequel, *Diggeth Thou?* beginning on page 207.

6. Burley here refers to the author Zora Neale Hurston. See pages 78–79 for the Hurston quotations and the editor's note that accompanies them for a reference citation.

7. Here and at other points throughout the text, Burley uses "glimmers" or "glim" to describe eyes and eyesight. Elsewhere, and in his accompanying glossary, he uses "gimmers" and "gim." This could have been a series of mistakes, but the common association of glimmering with eyesight (e.g., "the glimmer in her eye") suggests that the two spellings were interchangeable, even though "glimmers" and "glim" did not make it into Burley's glossary. In each instance, this text keeps Burley's original choice.

8. The definitions section originally following the text of the *Handbook* is, in this edition, at the close of the entire volume, begin-

ning on page 207, immediately following Burley's second work, *Diggeth Thou?*

9. The quoted passages come from Hurston's "Characteristics of Negro Expression," originally published in 1934 in a rare British anthology titled *Negro*. Wishart and Company originally published the collection compiled and edited by Nancy Cunard. Only a thousand were published, and many of those remained unsold. Though the volume was rare, the *New York Amsterdam News* received a review copy, most likely where Burley found the piece. See Nancy Cunard, ed., *Negro: An Anthology*, edited and abridged by Hugh Ford (New York: Frederick Ungar., 1970), 24–46.

10. "Charley" Barnet is actually Charlie Barnet. Charles Daly Barnet was one of the first white bandleaders to use black musicians, and he made his name largely through arrangements imitative of Duke Ellington. His work would best be described as big band swing, rather than improvisational jazz. The bulk of his recording success came between 1939 and 1944 (Barry Kernfeld, ed., *The New Grove Dictionary of Jazz*, vol. 1, A-K (New York: Macmillan, 1988), 73–74.

11. "All reet" is a modification of "all right," or the later "alright," a phrase used to indicate approval. The term was in use well before the *Handbook* appeared. Robert S. Gold's etymology traces it to the mid-1930s. Burley, however, interprets the adjectival phrase as a verb, even enunciating a tense structure for it. Whereas in mainstream English, tense change would come from the verb (e.g., "Mary is all right," "Mary was all right," Mary will be all right."), Burley changes the spelling of "reet" to mark time. The benefit of such a construction to the speaker in a language system based heavily on contraction, of course, is that the verb can be contracted in all tenses (e.g., "Mary's all reet," "Mary's all root," "Mary's all rote."). Jive, at least in this instance, is adapting to the needs of its speakers, not just their whims. Robert S. Gold, *A Jazz Lexicon* (New York: Alfred A. Knopf, 1964), 6-7, 247–248; and *Oxford English Dictionary*, 2nd ed., vol. 1 (Oxford: Clarendon Press, 1989), 347, 363.

12. Van Vechten's novel is a successful and sympathetic portrait of the Harlem jazz scene, though its sensational title generated a storm of controversy upon its initial publication in 1926. See Carl Van Vechten, *Nigger Heaven* (Urbana: University of Illinois Press, 2000).

13. The original text omits the definition of "slammer." It has been restored here using Burley's definition from the glossary.

14. Mencken did, in fact, include Burley's *Handbook* in the

"American Slang" section of his 1948 second supplement to the 1936 *The American Language*. He used the *Handbook* and Burley's "Back Door Stuff" for many of his examples and noted that Burley "has made many contributions to the vocabulary" (707). His overall depiction of jive, however, was less favorable. Mencken took issue with Conrad's introduction to the *Handbook*, arguing that any depiction of jive as somehow "revolutionary" was "a romantic exaggeration" (705). "The queer jargon called *jive*, which had its heyday in the early 1940s," writes Mencken, "was an amalgam of Negro slang from Harlem and the argots of drug addicts and the pettier sort of criminals, with occasional additions from the Broadway gossip columns and the high-school campus. It seems to have arisen at the start among jazz musicians, many of them Negroes and perhaps more of them addicts, and its chief users were always youthful devotees of the more delirious sort of ballroom dancing, i.e., the so-called *jitterbugs*" (704–5). H. L. Mencken, *Supplement II, The American Language: An Inquiry into the Development of English in the United States* (New York: Alfred A. Knopf, 1948), 704–7. The section on "American Slang" runs from 643 to 786.

15. The "Jive Dictionary" Burley refers to is the "Jiver's Bible" included at the close of the *Handbook*. In this edition, it follows both the *Handbook* and *Diggeth Thou?*

16. While Burley's claims here are probably a mixture of accuracy and bluster, in 2005 only fifteen American libraries claimed possession of the *Handbook*, in one form or another. Only two held *Diggeth Thou?*

Lightning Source UK Ltd.
Milton Keynes UK
UKHW040617010922
408166UK00006B/493